C000252386

'Brother Ramon was the sort of
point of orientation for all kinds c
integrity shows what the gospel actually looks like, and how thin
and pale most of our Christian practice is. It is a delight that he will,
through this book, be introduced to a new generation, and Canon
Arthur Howells deserves the warmest gratitude for his work, letting
us see something of Ramon's remarkable life as well as his writing
and teaching.'

Rowan Williams, Master of Magdalene College, Cambridge; McDonald Professor
in Christian Theology at St Mellitus College

'Arthur Howells is one of those remarkable, reliable and perceptive
priests... His writings and his edited collections of the writings
of others are always worth exploring... In this biography, his
appreciation of the many facets of the character of the charismatic
and spiritually engaging Ramon is hugely attractive. He charts
Ramon's life from its early and challenging beginnings in South
Wales through to its flourishing, across the ecumenical spectrum,
where he established himself as a much-loved and sought-after
teacher, guide and priest, always pointing others, not to himself, but
to Christ. I take huge pleasure in commending this book.'

John D.E. Davies, Archbishop of Wales and Bishop of Swansea and Brecon

'Brother Ramon was my friend; his interest, tall tales and forensic
prompting cheered and challenged me... This cheer and challenge
was familiar to many, and I am thrilled Arthur has brought that to
the page. This book makes Brother Ramon's example and message
clear: you don't have to join a religious order or become a hermit
to commune with God; rather, God inhabits your daily life, whatever
that is, and is available to be recognised at every turn. Brother
Ramon's life and work shows that true prayer – which transforms us
into alignment with the divine – becomes as imminent as breathing
when we notice our need and desire for God.'

Chris Powell, Group Analyst

The Bible Reading Fellowship
15 The Chambers, Vineyard
Abingdon OX14 3FE
brf.org.uk

The Bible Reading Fellowship (BRF) is a Registered Charity (233280)

ISBN 978 0 85746 662 4
First published 2018
10 9 8 7 6 5 4 3 2 1 0
All rights reserved

Acknowledgements
Unless otherwise acknowledged, scripture quotations are from The New Revised
Standard Version of the Bible, Anglicised edition, copyright © 1989, 1995 by the
Division of Christian Education of the National Council of the Churches of Christ in the
United States of America. Used by permission. All rights reserved.

Scripture quotations taken from The Holy Bible, New International Version (Anglicised
edition) copyright © 1979, 1984, 2011 by Biblica. Used by permission of Hodder &
Stoughton Publishers, a Hachette UK company. All rights reserved. 'NIV' is a registered
trademark of Biblica. UK trademark number 1448790.

Scripture quotations taken from the Holy Bible, English Standard Version, published
by HarperCollins Publishers, © 2001 Crossway Bibles, a division of Good News
Publishers. Used by permission. All rights reserved.

Scripture quotations from The Revised Standard Version of the Bible, copyright ©
1946, 1952, 1971 by the Division of Christian Education of the National Council of
the Churches of Christ in the United States of America. Used by permission. All rights
reserved.

Photos on pages 9 and 84 supplied by Brian and Jackie Lloyd; photo on page 113 by
Molly Dowell.

Every effort has been made to trace and contact copyright owners for material used
in this resource. We apologise for any inadvertent omissions or errors, and would
ask those concerned to contact us so that full acknowledgement can be made in
the future.

A catalogue record for this book is available from the British Library

Printed and bound by CPI Group (UK) Ltd, Croydon CR0 4YY

A Franciscan Way of Life

Brother Ramon's quest for holiness

ARTHUR HOWELLS

*To Doreen
with best wishes
Arthur*

April 2018

For Stan and Jenny,
my father and mother:
gratitude and love.

Acknowledgements

I am grateful to those who have helped me to tell the story of Ramon's life in this book. I would like to thank those who have read the manuscript and offered feedback: Ronald Powell, who also generously provided me with his letters from Ramon, Chris Powell, Ieuan Lloyd and John Howells. I am also grateful to Kathleen Boyce for sharing her ideas with me for using the anthology as a means of questioning and reflection. Mike Parsons and the staff at The Bible Reading Fellowship have been most encouraging and helpful. Finally, I am indebted to Canon David Winter for writing the Foreword.

Contents

Foreword 7

— LIFE —   9

By way of introduction 10

Early days 13

Conversion 18

Pacifism 21

The student 26

The Baptist minister 27

Becoming an Anglican 29

The quest for a solitary life 31

The Franciscan 39

On the Lleyn 49

The Tymawr years 57

The hermitage at Glasshampton 65

The great 'Hullo'! 73

— LETTERS —   85

Journeys in faith: the pilgrimage 114

Praying and reflecting: meditation 123

Alone with God: solitude 140

Living faith: in the world 155

Books by Brother Ramon...169

Notes..171

Foreword

This book is about an extraordinary man, Raymond Lloyd, best known by his later title as Brother Ramon. It describes his spiritual journey, from eloquent and effective evangelist and Baptist pastor in his native South Wales, to his discovery of Franciscan spirituality and eventually to the life of a hermit. The second half of his life was lived in a sequence of solitary dwellings: first a remote cottage in Wales, then a caravan in the West Country and finally a hut in the grounds of the Franciscan community at Glasshampton.

Some people seem natural 'hermits', but Ramon (the name he adopted as a friar) was certainly not. He loved conversation, laughter and company. He was gregarious and charming. Yet he found in this discipline of solitude and silence a depth of relationship with God that outweighed for him all the apparent social and human deprivation. Those who knew him well were compelled to admit that, although the discipline was hard and he did have days of acute loneliness, he was, as a person and as a Christian, a man who found his whole life utterly fulfilling.

This book tells his story, truthfully and frankly. For those of us whose Christian path has followed other ways, or who cannot understand why a person of his gifts as preacher and evangelist should spend his life in a remote shelter, the story is a revelation of the miracle of the ways of God with people. From that hut came book after book of the most profound but accessible spiritual wisdom, an opening of the Bible's deepest truths and a message for those who find the road hard and steep. A chapter or two of Ramon could be a transforming experience.

Although I 'knew' him, I never met him. After all, he was a hermit! But a couple of times a year he permitted himself the liberty of a visit to Swansea to spend time with his sister – and there was a telephone. The hermit and I would chat away, and also wrestle sometimes with issues that were troubling us. Then Ramon would return to his hermitage (always travelling by thumbing lifts, to the occasional great blessing of the drivers). His was a remarkable life, and this book – both the story and the extracts from his writings – is a splendid celebration of it.

David Winter

LIFE

By way of introduction

I doubt whether it had ever happened before, or since. There within the walls of Canterbury Cathedral at a traditional choral evensong on a summer's Sunday evening, a Franciscan friar ascended the pulpit and announced the text for his sermon by singing with gusto 'Love Divine, all loves excelling'. His voice echoed around those ancient walls, soaring up to the roof and, when the singing was over and there was a pause for breath, the congregation waited in hushed expectancy for what was to follow. The preacher was Brother Ramon of the Anglican Society of St Francis, and this was his introduction to a sermon on the feast of John and Charles Wesley. What better way to begin than by singing one of Charles Wesley's famous hymns? From then on, without so much as a note in front of him, our preacher challenged us, taught us, stimulated us and entertained us with a vigorous sermon sprinkled liberally with anecdotes. It was delivered with a conviction that demanded our attention and left us in no doubt that we needed men and women of the calibre and evangelistic zeal of these founders of Methodism to proclaim the gospel today.

I believe that every member of that congregation was inspired by what they heard that Sunday evening. I had no opportunity of speaking to Ramon after that service, but later I met him and over the years we became close friends. Indeed, it was only when we gathered for his requiem at Worcester Cathedral that my wife and I discovered that we were among many hundreds who had a similar relationship with him. And they came from all walks of life as well as from differing Christian traditions. A few were members of other faiths, among them a Hindu nurse who had cared for him in his last days.

In this short book, I attempt to introduce Ramon to those who did not know him, while reminding those who did know him of his loveable character and personality. He had a tremendous influence on so many people; he radiated the love of Christ, not only by what he said and wrote but by who he was. He possessed that rare quality of complete trustfulness. You knew that you could depend on him to give you sound advice, and that when he promised to pray for you he would indeed keep that promise. He was truly interested in you and your family, your work and all with which you were involved. He had a phenomenal memory for names and out of the blue would recall an incident or something you had shared with him many years ago.

His exuberant personality, his uninhibited joy and his breathless energy were infectious. His humour was almost childlike and, wherever he was, there was laughter and fun. He could mimic and tease. He had a fund of stories for every occasion and he shared his life openly and generously with all with whom he came into contact – with old and new friends, children, the young and the old, the lorry driver, the university student, the shop assistant or the office clerk. A casual acquaintance in a short time became a friend. A lorry driver giving him a lift would soon pour out his difficulties and problems, for the brown habit was no barrier as the jovial wearer frequently laughed at himself and the newly found friend warmed to him. He had this extraordinary quality of listening intently and discerning precisely what needed to be said, and of encouraging people to share their fears and, above all, to know that God loved them.

There was a boyishness about him as he excitedly immersed himself in the God-created world. Like Francis, he recognised God in the natural world around him and gave him praise from his heart. He always left you with the impression that he discovered God everywhere. He loved the Gower coast, which he had explored as a young boy. On one occasion, we visited the isolated little parish church of Llandewi where, after a while, a bird flew in and was trapped. Despite our efforts to free it, we failed and had to leave it behind locked doors. Ramon was quite upset by this incident and the following day was anxious to know if it had escaped.

This is by no means a complete biography. Unfortunately, I have been unable to discover many of his unpublished works or his journal. We know that he destroyed most of the letters he had written when he entered the hermit life, but I am grateful to Ron Powell, a very close friend of his from college days, for allowing me to reproduce here some of the correspondence that he had with Ramon. These letters, together with extracts from some of his books, give us a picture of this gentle, saintly priest and friar whose life was one long search for holiness. I hope also that the extracts from his books will give readers an appetite to read them in their entirety.

Early days

'The ugly, lovely town of Swansea' with 'a museum that should have been in a museum' was how Dylan Thomas, a contemporary of Ramon, described their home town. As a flourishing port and a major centre for heavy industry, Swansea reached its zenith in the 18th and 19th centuries. By the mid-19th century, it had become the largest exporter of coal in the world, but its success came at a great price. Scarred by waste deposits, poisoned land, polluted air and more than its fair share of dirt and grime, it was the industrialists who benefited most from its economic prosperity. The town centre was completely obliterated in a three-nights blitz in 1943. Recovery was slow and it is perhaps true to say that it is only now in the early decades of the 21st century that the city is beginning to have a new lease of life.

Raymond Lloyd, for 'Ramon' was his monastic name, was born on 13 October 1936 at Baptist Well Street, just a few minutes' walk from Swansea's city centre. He was brought up in what was then a poorer part of the town, a neighbourhood where the workers in the local industries lived in a rather shabby area called ironically 'Waun Wen' (trans. 'White Meadow'). However, the colourless surroundings were compensated for by a strong sense of community. This was a place where the front doors of the terraced houses were open day and night, visitors were made welcome, the 'front room' was reserved for funerals or the visit of rather more distinguished guests like the vicar or the minister and for special occasions of celebration – Christmas and birthdays. The kitchen was where the family lived, while the back door led out to a small yard where the coal was stored and a small lean-to housed the lavatory, the '*Ty Bach*' (trans. 'little house'). In such close-knit communities, relatives were never far away while adopted 'uncles' and 'aunties' were countless. It was in this homely atmosphere that the young Raymond spent his childhood years.

He presents us with the picture of himself as a rather lonely boy surrounded by the love of his parents, David and Edna. On his own admission, he describes himself as being rather independent in thought and action, shy, quiet and unsure of himself. This is why he needed that love and understanding in which he could feel secure. Undoubtedly, the seeds of his love for people were sown in this intimate family circle, for it is obvious that his parents had a great capacity for love. The family circle was complete when, at the age of eleven, his sister Wendy was born. Writing about his parents, he says:

My mother was a sanguine personality, much given to humorous mischief, laughter and sharing with many talkative friends and family. She was extrovert, optimistic, outgoing and never still. My father and she had shared poverty and difficult times together, but she always saw the bright side, surmounted obstacles, overcame her illnesses and displayed enormous vitality and joy.

My father had a melancholic streak, little conversation and lived mainly within himself. He had few real friends and, with no real opportunities, had many unfulfilled hopes and untried or unsuccessful schemes. He had a profound though hidden sense of the mystery of human life, which he found difficult to articulate, and although we got on very well together it was only during the last decade of his life that he shared with me his joys and fears. There were times when we wept together during conversations in the last few years, and they remain very precious to me.[1]

Raymond inherited some of those distinctive qualities that each of his parents possessed in his own character. That outgoing, talkative mother and the more silent father found their way into the personality of their son.

Many years later, Raymond would come back to Swansea every August to visit his family. He would meet his friend, Ron Powell, for walks, and would make arrangements to take his mum and dad out. Ron describes them as:

> … lovely, simple souls so proud of Raymond. It was such a revelation to find a boy like him so academic coming from a humble home and a loving family. He knew just what his parents would appreciate: a pint in the Pier [Hotel] in Mumbles for Dad, and for his mum a handful of coins for the nearby fruit machines. We would leave them there for an hour or so and collect them later.

On one occasion, Ron picked them up to take them to Glasshampton, where Ramon proudly introduced them to all the brothers and then at Evensong in the chapel would give a simple homily based on a children's hymn his mum would remember from Sunday school days.

In an article which he wrote on 'Hermit Friendship' for the *Franciscan* in 1998, he outlines what friendship means for him and particularly its impingement on his hermit life. In solitariness, he admits the need for friendship as he tells of his boyhood:

> I was basically shy and tentative in reaching out to others, so I would cycle down the coast road in Swansea to the Mumbles cliff path. There I would chain the bike and go wandering around the edge of the sea into the sandy bays, and act out my friendship towards the mystery which I felt was dwelling within and flowing from earth, sea and sky, and particularly within the scariness of the caves.[2]

It is apparent that school was not the happiest place for young Raymond, for there his gentle, quiet qualities made him a target for bullies, who were ready to take advantage of those who tended to be shy and gentle. He tells us about 'The Black Spot Gang', so called because of the indelible black spot which they had marked on their wrists and was hidden under their sleeves. The unfortunates who had no black spot were mercilessly 'done over'. As he didn't belong to this gang, he joined a smaller, rival group which indulged in smoking and swearing, but this was not his scene either, and unsurprisingly, when he was converted, it was something he distanced himself from. He now found that not only had he a change of mind and heart, but he also possessed a new strength to meet opposition with boldness and courage. He could not be persuaded to join a group whose actions he found abhorrent and out of tune with his Christian principles. For him, smoking and swearing were 'out'.

After attending Waun Wen and Mayhill Schools, he went on to Hafod Senior School. Here, he was unsuccessful in passing the eleven plus examination, which was the qualification for entry into the grammar school. The only alternative was to receive secondary education at a private establishment. At the age of 13, he obtained a part scholarship allowing him to be a student at Greggs Commercial College. Here, he learned shorthand, which he was to find so useful in years to come. His parents, however, found it increasingly difficult to pay the fees so Raymond took on a paper round on weekdays and worked in a butcher's stall in Swansea Market on Saturdays. In spite of these efforts, at the beginning of one term, there was a shortfall. It looked as if Raymond would be unable to continue his education. However, unknown to himself and his father, his mother pawned her wedding ring. They would have been none the wiser had not his father discovered the pawn ticket in a drawer in their bedroom upstairs. His father was furious. The truth emerged, the ring was retrieved and a generous deacon at the church paid the fees. Raymond was truly amazed at his parents' acts of self-sacrifice, which he never forgot. In his writing, he speaks frequently not only of their generosity but of their love.

> Because of their love I was able to recognise the love of God in Jesus when I was twelve years of age and began to love him then. The mingling in my life of love human and divine have enabled me to be open to the world of nature and to all things good and true and life-giving, for I have always seen them as manifestations of love.

… the openness to love is openness to life. St John of the Cross said that where there is no love you should pour love in, and then you would draw love out. And he wrote these lovely words: 'When the evening of this life comes we shall be judged by love.'[3]

Conversion

From an early age, Raymond had attended the local Tabernacle Baptist Chapel in Waun Wen. Here at Sunday school, he became familiar with those choruses which he later sang so heartily, loved so much and quoted repeatedly. As a result of the teaching, he immersed himself in the scriptures. In his tribute to him at his requiem in Worcester Cathedral, Ieuan Lloyd said:

> I first met Ramon when he came to my father's mission hall in Morriston in the 50s. His enthusiasm, his exuberance could be overpowering. At the time, he was an active banner carrier and had a verse of scripture on his swimming trunks. That enthusiasm took a different form but, as we all know, it remained with him all his life.

One evening, he went along with some friends to a special missionary service in the chapel to listen to a group of young people in their 20s speak with fervour, excitement and enthusiasm about their experiences of God. They had heard the call of Christ to service and had made their response regardless of the consequences. We can imagine the young Raymond, bright and intelligent, seeking for a deeper relationship with God and finding at this meeting just what he was looking for. The atmosphere would have been electric. The sound of those well-known gospel songs and choruses would ring in his ears. The message of the gospel came through to him loud and clear and the sincerity of the young men was indisputable and tangible. He was captivated. In his own words:

> The whole theme of that service was call, challenge, decision for Christ; it was one of those rare moments when the time of decision was upon me. I felt a deeply emotional surge of response which carried me forward to a simple prayer of

surrender to Christ, mingled with tears of joy. Again, I could not have put it into words, but it was a moment of both heart and mind; for from that time there has been no looking back, only a deepening of commitment, a maturing of experience, a widening of horizons. All of these are grounded in that simple, biblical and evangelical experience of conversion and baptism within the fellowship of the church. I was committed now. At home, at school, there was no doubt where I stood.[4]

The more sophisticated would dismiss this kind of experience in one so young as an adolescent 'blip' which could be expected to disappear with maturity. This was certainly not the case, for throughout his life and ministry Raymond frequently refers to this incident as a turning point in his life. He was convinced that on that day he had been truly converted, that he had actually been 'born again' and as a result his life took a radical change of direction. He was filled with an evangelical zeal to communicate and proclaim Christ there and then, something he was to do so effectively for the rest of his life through the spoken and written word. He now possessed an infectious enthusiasm for the things of God. His shyness seemed to be a thing of the past. He could face up to the bullying he had suffered at Hafod School. His relationship with Christ brought with it a resilience and courage, together with a fervour which nothing could dampen.

In *A Hidden Fire*, he speaks further about the consequences of this experience:

This experience brought to the fore an ability to share and communicate which I had only feebly understood previously. From age twelve to sixteen, I tentatively began to sing and pray publicly and even to take part in the devotional services and young people's work of the church. I was friendly, during this time, with groups of other Christians, some from the Pentecostal movement, and they spoke freely of an experience of the Holy Spirit which again sent me searching the pages of the New Testament.[5]

He now became an avid reader of the New Testament. Much of it he learned by heart, for he had a phenomenal memory. Reading the Acts of the Apostles, he discovered the fundamental importance of the work of the Holy Spirit in the lives of those first Christians and, at the age of 16, had a further experience which he describes thus:

> In a group prayer meeting in an upper room, I experienced an overwhelming experience of the Holy Spirit. It burned itself into the depths of my being, bringing with it an inebriation, freedom and emotional release which crowned my childhood and turned my shyness into boldness, courage and enthusiasm for God. It was an experience which was accompanied by the gift of tongues, and I found, some time ago, the old, tattered diary which says that I could hardly walk in a straight line to get home, and that the inebriation lasted six weeks, resulting in bringing five young people to commitment to Christ.[6]

As we observe his life, it becomes obvious that these spiritual experiences had a profound effect on him. After the charismatic experience, he tells us of the outpouring of joy and thanksgiving which ensued, which he can only compare with the apostles' experience at Pentecost – something that captivated his mind as well as his heart. As time went on, his reading was no longer confined to the writings of evangelical theologians. It became much broader: Brother Lawrence, St Augustine, St John of the Cross and many other Catholic writers now featured in his studies. He also began to think ecumenically and to appreciate that there was much to learn from other Christian traditions with which up until then he had been unfamiliar. It was through this new stimulus that he probably came to know something about the monastic tradition.

Pacifism

In 1947, the government passed the National Service act. Healthy men aged 18 or over were obliged to serve in the armed forces for 18 months. Prior to his 18th birthday, the time came for Raymond to register. Conscription came as a significant test of his faith and conviction. By nature, he was a peaceable man who could not imagine taking up arms and fighting and killing other men in war. Christ was in reality for him the Prince of Peace and, if it was a question of taking sides, then he was on his side – that of a peacemaker.

Before, however, refusing to sign on for military service, he had to wrestle with what effect this would have on his parents. He knew that they would find it hard to sympathise with the views of a son who was a conscientious objector. The very word 'conchie', much used in common parlance, was a word of derision. Pacifists, however conscientious and sincere, were not to be tolerated in a society which feared the tyrannical oppression of the enemy and had witnessed in recent years the pain and suffering that war brought with it.

There were many ex-servicemen and women living in the community who would have vivid memories of the suffering and death of comrades and friends in the war, and there were also those who would recall the destruction of the town and many of its neighbouring communities in the three-night blitz on Swansea in February 1941. Not to take up arms was nothing less than cowardice in the eyes of ordinary people. To be a pacifist was to step back from one's duty. It was unpatriotic and disloyal: something that could only bring shame to the relatives and friends of the person involved. Raymond graphically describes his reaction when notice of his need to register, which was not unexpected, arrived:

> I picked up the envelope from the doormat and my heart turned over, because I had thought about it, debated the matter with myself and a few friends and knew quite clearly what I must do.[7]

He knew that, however unpleasant the outcome would be and in spite of opposition from his parents and friends, there could be no compromise. His views received no sympathy from his confidant and friend, his Baptist minister, who himself had served as a chaplain in the RAF and looked back at his time in the services as a glorious opportunity to witness for Christ in a unique way. The young Raymond knew that he had to take a lonely and unpopular stand and the best way forward seemed to be to register for a non-combatant unit.

At the local labour exchange in the centre of the town on the prescribed day, Raymond Lloyd joined the queue of those of the same age, some of them school friends, many of whom, despite having no Christian convictions, were equally hesitant when it came to signing on the dotted line to commit themselves to military service. When his turn came, he advanced over the brown lino floor to the green baize-covered steel desk behind which a uniformed official was seated, waiting with pen poised to fill in his registration form. The first question was no problem. He gave his name, address and date of birth and then:

Clerk For which service do you state a preference?

Me Oh, RAF I think – but I want to serve in a non-combatant unit.

Clerk You'll go where you are put.

Me No, I'm sorry, but I want to serve in a non-combatant unit.

Clerk We tell you – you don't tell us.

Me   Look, I'm sorry but I *do* feel strongly about this, and
I can't go into a combatant unit.

At this, the clerk lost his cool and got edgy – he'd been
registering lads all the morning, and probably was fed-up with
this repetitive job. There was a queue behind me, and he told
me in clear language that I would do what I was told.

Me   No I won't do that. There must be a way to get into a
non-combatant unit – what do I have to do?

Clerk You have to be a conscientious objector.

Me   Well, no one told me that. (*turning to the lads in the
queue*) Did you know that?

But no one would look at me directly, let alone answer me.
I suddenly felt alone. I need not have felt like that, because
if I had maintained my clear conviction, I would then have
experienced what came later: an overwhelming sense of God's
presence. In a few moments of time, I heard the interior voice
which said: 'You have seen where compromise has led you.
If you had done what you knew you ought to do, you would
not be in this mess now. But it's not too late – if you will take
your stand.' And immediately I knew what I should do, and this
'infusion' of the necessary strength was given. And so:

Me   Look, I've said I'm sorry, but now I know what I should
do. Not only will I not serve in a combatant unit,
but I will not serve at all. I want to register as an
unqualified conscientious objector… I'm not going
to sign your form, and unless you register me as a
conscientious objector, I am going to leave now.

I remember, quite clearly, the quiet and deliberate manner in
which I spoke, and the half-turn I took, though I had butterflies
in my tummy. But now there was nothing which could shake
me – it was *contra mundum* again and, if the firing squad had
been there, I would have maintained my stand. This taught
me a great deal about myself, and about what had happened

to me over the five years since my conversion. Suddenly the clerk sighed, realised now what he had on his hands, looked squarely at me (did I detect a wry smile?), and said:

Clerk   Come back! (*silence*) Name please![8]

On his return home, his mother and father reacted in a way that did not surprise him. His father was rather angry, impatient and irritated with the stance his son had taken, while his mother in despair said, 'What will the neighbours say?' and immediately went out to do some shopping. She was soon back and fully reassured, for her neighbours had told her that they were not surprised. They had expected Raymond to uphold his principles as a conscientious objector. He was soon to discover that his friends were equally unsurprised. One of them had even prayed for this result.

Three months later came a further test. This involved a trip to Cardiff to appear before the customary tribunal presided over by Judge Ernest Evans. Raymond was one of about a dozen conscientious objectors who now had to state their case. At seventeen and a half, he had prayerfully considered what he would say, imagining the type of questions he would be asked. One question which he was prepared to answer and expected to be asked was how he would react if the enemy broke into his home and threatened his parents and his sister. He had thought this through, as he knew that this would be an inevitable question. Present at the tribunal was a Quaker lady, a newspaper reporter. They soon engaged in conversation and she was full of admiration for his courage and promised to pray for him. Well into her 60s, she was fully aware of the cost of conscience on the part of the young men appearing before the tribunal. In the witness box, Raymond answered the questions put to him clearly and courteously and, before the interview ended, the very question for which he had prepared was asked:

Judge   Tell me, do you have parents, brothers and sisters?

Me   Yes, parents and one sister.

Judge Now, suppose your home was broken into in time of war. Your parents and sister threatened and beaten. Would you stand by and let it happen?

Me I cannot tell you, sir, what I would do in such circumstances, but the Christ who stands by me now in this dock will be standing by me then, and he will show me what to do.

Judge Do you really believe that?

Me Yes, I do.[9]

It was obvious that Raymond's sincerity and integrity could not be disputed and his testimony was accepted by the judge. The Quaker lady's prayers had been answered, and he would be happy to spend the next two years in farming, mining, agriculture or medical work as many objectors to war service did. As it happened, he became a state registered nurse (SRN) for three years, working conscientiously and diligently in the nearby Morriston Hospital. Two years were obligatory, but he stayed on for a further year.

Brother Austin tells this story of Ramon's continuing and steadfast opposition to war:

We were due to have General Sir Hugh Beech (third Order SSF) come and lecture on being a Christian in the forces. Ramon was a militant pacifist and threatened to have a banner denouncing the event as Beech arrived. This sent Brother Bernard, the Guardian, into panic and Ramon asked me about it and I persuaded him to forget the banner and stay and ask Beech hard questions at the discussion. Both powerful minds and great good were done for peace that day!

The student

The year 1960 saw Raymond Lloyd as student secretary in the South Wales Baptist College in Cardiff where he was training for the ministry. He was a hard and conscientious worker. A fellow student recalls him hastily leaving the lecture hall and making straight for his room to type his notes up. Academically, he was brilliant. While respected for his convictions, he was, as one of his contemporaries put it in a tribute to him in the *Baptist Times*, 'regarded as an eccentric, fervent, faithful Pentecostal evangelical whose active service for Christ involved him in so many activities not least the carrying of a scripture banner through the streets of Cardiff and Swansea as an evangelical endeavour'.[10]

Another said of him: 'To be with Raymond Lloyd was to be with an evangelical whirlwind. Whether charging through Cardiff on a Saturday, Bible text banner aloft, or holding kids entranced at an open-air meeting, or preaching with gusto at a youth rally, no one could doubt his passion for Christ.'[11]

The Voice, a Swansea weekly newspaper, has an article about 'Mr Raymond Lloyd', who is described as a young man of 23 who had a conversion experience and seeks to share his faith with young people 'who do not know Christ'. He is pictured with a banner in one hand and a Bible in the other.[12] The writer goes on to say: 'We can think what we like about the advantage of text-carrying, but we have to admire the courage and conviction of those who do it.'

The Baptist minister

After his ordination to the Baptist ministry, Raymond served his first pastorate at Grangetown in Cardiff. Subsequently, he moved to further study at the International Baptist Theological Seminary at Rüschlikon, Zurich. He travelled lightly. He had given away his records, equipment and furniture and carried all his possessions in one small suitcase. At Zurich, he gained his MTh *cum laude*. The treatise he submitted as part of the requirements for his degree was: 'The concept of God in Bishop John Robinson: A critical study of the sources and distinctiveness'. John Robinson (1919–83) was Bishop of Woolwich and a New Testament scholar who reached notoriety when his book, *Honest to God*, was published in 1963. This was a radical approach to the traditional concept of God which caused a furore among Catholic and Evangelical theologians alike and resulted in a wide discussion and debate by Christians and non-Christians as it challenged the orthodox view. It was a turning point in Raymond's theology. There is a telling statement towards the end of his treatise where he says:

> We maintain that we must continue to work within the theistic framework, but Robinson has showed us, perhaps indirectly, that unless our concept of God 'relates' experientially to modern man, then our preaching and faith will not communicate.[13]

During the summer of 1968, while home on vacation, Raymond was introduced to the members of Sardis Baptist Church in Resolven, a small village in the Vale of Neath once surrounded by a number of industrial works. Ron Powell's father was senior deacon and lay pastor during the interregnum. He and his wife had a great affection for Ramon. Later, when Ramon was appointed their pastor, Mrs Powell would cook him a huge breakfast on those mornings when he had arranged some early morning prayer times which often included

Communion. (This would be quite an innovation in a Baptist church, where traditionally Communion was celebrated once a month on 'Communion Sunday'.)

As a student, for a short time he led a series of Bible studies on Thursday evenings and often officiated and preached on Sundays. At this time, the members were searching for a new pastor while Raymond, too, was seeking guidance for his future. Soon an agreement was reached and he accepted the invitation to become their minister with the proviso that it would be a short-term arrangement lasting no longer than twelve months. He began his ministry in June of the following year and remained until July 1970. One of the congregation writes:

> Raymond lived in the church manse and became very well known in the village. His friendly, happy nature endeared him to everyone and his pastorate was like a breath of fresh air. He encouraged people into a deeper walk with God, teaching much about prayer and how to come closer to God. His departure was a sad time for us all.

During this period, Ron was the minister of Mumbles Baptist Church and he and Raymond would meet up for regular walks in Gower. They shared confidences, and Ron recalls his friend telling him that he felt drawn to one of the Anglican religious orders. Ron himself had considered becoming an Anglican and it was he who introduced Raymond to Cerne Abbas (Hilfield), the mother house of the Franciscans where he himself had made many retreats. In the decision he was about to make, Raymond had one stumbling block. How was he going to break the news to Mr Powell senior, whom he held in great regard, that he intended to become an Anglican? But he need not have worried. Mr Powell had seen it coming in Raymond's subtle change of emphasis both in his preaching and in the way he conducted worship.

Becoming an Anglican

Ramon left Sardis and the Baptist ministry to become an Anglican. He was attracted by its liturgy and the whole ethos of the tradition, and frequently visited parish churches and cathedrals to experience structured worship and to wonder at the beauty and awesomeness of so many of these ancient buildings. It was while visiting St Gabriel's Church in Brynmill, Swansea, a church steeped in the Anglo-Catholic tradition, that he met the curate, James Coutts, and asked to be confirmed. His confirmation by Rt Revd J.J.A. Thomas, the Bishop of Swansea and Brecon, took place at St Gabriel's in 1970 and was attended by several members of Sardis who continued to keep in touch with him throughout his ministry and were subsequently present at the requiem for him which took place at the same St Gabriel's shortly after his funeral.

After his funeral, I met a Baptist minister who had been invited by Raymond to make a retreat at Glasshampton. A monastery was unfamiliar territory to him and it was with some trepidation that he arrived at what was to be his home for a few days. After unpacking, he made his way to the chapel where he discovered that shortly a service was to take place. 'Evensong and Benediction' the notice said.[14] Evensong he was familiar with, but Benediction?

The bell rang and at the appointed time he made his way to the chapel and took his seat at the back. Evensong came to an end and he suddenly found himself surrounded by clouds of incense, while the altar was resplendent with flickering candles and an officiating priest emerged in a golden cope. The brother kneeling alongside him whispered in his ear: 'Not very Baptist this, is it?' and added, 'Come to think of it, not very Anglican either!' That was Raymond. He was not averse to a little ceremonial and certainly the centrality of the Eucharist was important to him. Even when alone at his hermitage, he would always celebrate the Eucharist on Sundays, making it the focal point not only of the day, but of the whole week.

While becoming an Anglican must have been quite a shock for his Christian friends, they would have understood that this move was not a spur-of-the-moment decision. They knew Raymond better than that, and would be aware that this was something that he had struggled with and prayed about before taking the final step. He certainly had no regrets and neither did he leave behind him the rich tradition of evangelicalism which had been so much a part of his life. His evangelistic fervour never diminished and he spoke proudly of the broadness and inclusiveness of the Anglican Church, with its balance of word and sacrament which attracted him. However, he continued to be at home with a variety of Christian traditions, always respecting the other's point of view while also accepting the beauty of diversity of difference. In the tribute at his funeral, his friend Ieuan Lloyd said of him:

> One unique feature of his Christian life was that he had attended and preached in all branches of the Christian church. And so with his warm and open manner only, he was able to replace bigotry and prejudice with tolerance and understanding. He could get Anglo-Catholics to sing Elim choruses and a conference of Baptist ministers to handle a rosary.

The quest for a solitary life

In the autumn of 1976, Raymond was invited to a Hermits Symposium attended by hermits from Orthodox, Roman and Anglican traditions. The venue was St David's. The organisers could not have chosen a better place than this picturesque spot at the westernmost tip of West Wales, where St David (Dewi Sant) founded a monastery in the sixth century. Vallis Rosina (*Glyn Rhosyn* in Welsh), 'the valley of the little marsh', was similar to those deserted and waste places, many of them on the surrounding islands, where Celtic Christians would seek solitude in order to pursue lives dedicated to God. The primitive wooden huts which were built for Dewi Sant and his brothers are far removed from the magnificent cathedral which now stands on the site and is believed to house the relics of the saint himself. He was an ascetic reputed to have stood for long periods in cold water to subdue the flesh – an example to the members of the monastic community which he founded. He expected his monks to pray and to study and to spend time each day in hard manual labour.

This site, hallowed by almost a thousand years of Christian devotion, continues to be a place of pilgrimage offering hospitality and welcome to the hordes of visitors who flock there. The atmosphere was right for such a gathering of hermits and others who were interested in the solitary life. Raymond had vivid memories of each day of the symposium from the early morning Eucharist in the sun-filled Lady Chapel, close to St David's reliquary where, as dawn broke, they sang the hymn 'Christ, whose glory fills the skies', to lectures on Celtic monasticism which concluded with long silences:

> The sense of corporate sharing in the great tradition of prayer was powerful, and the veil between earth and heaven was thin.[15]

Such corporate silence plumbed the depths of the love of God for him. Raymond immersed himself in this and emerged, even at this early period in his ministry, fully convinced that the way of contemplation lived out in the solitary life of the hermit was the direction to which God was calling him. It seems that this was not only what he had been looking for, but the path along which God was guiding him. He was fully aware of the sacrifices involved, of the loneliness which he would encounter and the darkness that might eventually engulf him but, once the decision was made, there would be no turning back. (We need to remember that this event took place on the eve of his entering the Franciscan community and that there would be many discussions with his spiritual directors before he took the necessary steps towards the hermit life.) One of the lectures on the hermit life at the symposium was given by Canon A.M. Allchin. Here, he comments on the challenge of the life:

> The life is one which demands considerable maturity, human and psychological, as well as ascetic and spiritual. It is not a way to be undertaken unadvisedly, lightly or wantonly,[16] and it will not ordinarily be undertaken without some considerable experience of a regular life of prayer and obedience lived in community.[17]

These words would have resonance for Raymond: a warning to those who would attempt to live the hermit life without preparation and experience of community living. There is nothing novel about solitude, as he would discover. Romantics may enthuse about living in a hut away from people, being self-sufficient and 'green', but in reality, it was not all sunshine. The winter, especially in bare and waste places, brings rain and wind, ice and snow, and the walls of a caravan or a wooden hut, as Raymond would discover, are thin and fragile, providing minimum shelter and little comfort. Hut living demands a wealth of both physical and spiritual resources. You have to be strong to survive!

The symposium at St David's came at the right time. Raymond had been trained at the Baptist College in Cardiff and was ordained as a Baptist minister prior to further training to be an Anglican priest, a parish priest and a member of the chaplaincy team at Glasgow University. He also served as a curate at the cathedral. It had been a busy life, sometimes of his own choosing rather hectic, as he hints in *Fullness of Joy*:

> My interior life was not keeping up with my busy schedule, and I realised like many busy parish priests and workers that I didn't have enough depth and experience to back up my preaching and teaching. Something had to be done. For some years I had been drawn to the 'religious life', but didn't envisage a contemplative community – I thought I was more of a friar than a monk.[18]

And a friar he became! His first choice was The Society of St John the Evangelist, founded in 1912 by an Anglican priest, Father Benson, a community keeping the Benedictine Rule with its mother house at Cowley, Oxford. The other possibility was The Society of St Francis, which had several houses scattered throughout England (and at that time one in Llandudno in North Wales). Raymond does not tell us why he chose the Franciscan way of life. Had he already met with some of the members of the Franciscan community or had he perhaps visited a Franciscan friary? Certainly in choosing to enter the Franciscan Order he would realise that he would be allowed more freedom to use his talents here than if he had chosen the more traditional monastic life. That freedom at this stage in his life was important to him, for it meant that he would be able to continue to use his communication skills, which he regarded as a gift from God, in preaching, teaching and leading missions – work which he loved and enjoyed – while the cloistered life of a monastery might have restrained him from using to the full that God-given energy and enthusiasm which overflowed from his personality. Later in his life of contemplation this would change, but his vocation to the Religious Life had to start somewhere and this was the choice he made. In *The Heart of Prayer,* he speaks movingly of the influence of St Francis:

I fell in love with Jesus, as did St Francis and the early Franciscan fools for Christ, though I did not come to know of them until some time later. The reason why I have been drawn into the Franciscan life is because of this very thing, for above all, Francis was a lover of Christ. He was also many other things, but his life and death are inexplicable without the centrality of the living, dying, risen Jesus. And the marks of the stigmata upon his body were but physical manifestations of the wounds of Jesus within his heart – wounds of love, compassion and service to the world.[19]

And again, in *Franciscan Spirituality*:

The whole meaning of discipline and asceticism in the life of Francis was the outcome of his love for Jesus. His simplicity and poverty was the bringing of his life into conformity with the way of Jesus. It was not asceticism for asceticism's sake, or poverty as an antidote to luxury and waste, or even as a rebuke to a worldly and luxurious Church or state, but a living out of the simplicity and discipline of a follower of Jesus.

If Francis wanted his friars and sisters to follow the way of his Rule, it was because the Rule embodied the gospel and was given him by God, and because he could say with St Paul: 'Be imitators of me, as I am of Christ.'[20]

Prior to committing himself as a Franciscan, Ramon had a year's experience of the discipline of the Religious Life as a member of the Community of the Transfiguration in Scotland. He joined this community in the New Year of 1970 and was professed as a novice on 13 September.

The Community was founded by Roland Walls in 1965, a priest of the Episcopal Church in Scotland. It was based at Roslyn (sometimes spelt Roslin) in the Pentland Hills to the south of Edinburgh. On the edge of the village is Roslyn Chapel, which is associated with the

Holy Grail, the cup which was reputed to have been used by Jesus at the Last Supper. In 2003, this became famous when Dan Brown included the legend in his *Da Vinci Code*. Father Roland Walls had been priest in charge of the chapel since 1962. The small community, which never exceeded five in number, was based in a refurbished, corrugated, ex-village institute with five or six huts in the enclosed garden. Raymond's hut measured only 8 x 6 feet. Bound by the traditional vows of poverty, chastity and obedience, the brethren led a strict life of prayer and work. Their constitution was based on the rules of St Benedict and St Francis. Some had full-time jobs which meant that they were not always able to be present in the chapel for the formal services. In spite of this, the daily round of Eucharist and praying the Divine Office was ceaselessly maintained. But this was not only a spiritual house. The homeless and displaced always found welcome and hospitality here. Roland Walls' obituary in *The Scotsman* gives us some idea of character of the community which Raymond joined:

> Here [at Roslyn] was not only a community that was ecumenical and open to all, but one which was able to reaffirm the value of the discarded and the decayed, an oasis of reality with no telephone or television. Before he retired Brother John – an Anglican priest and then Prior of the house – worked as a labourer in a local garage stripping down cars for repainting. Fr Roland, an Anglican priest for more than 40 years, had the gift of prising people open with the challenge of his humour and insight.[21]

Raymond tells us that those days in Roslin were extremely spartan.[22] He recalls waking up on a winter's morning with a coating of frost on his blanket, but the hut life and the ascetic discipline was a good preparation for what was to follow. Here in the Scottish Episcopal tradition, with the Celtic simplicity of the chapel hut and the ongoing rhythm of the daily Eucharist and Offices, he received a thorough grounding in the gospel life which was to undergird him for the rest of his life. It was here that he had a taste of hut dwelling. However, the huts which he erected later on at Glasshampton were a little larger than those at Roslyn. He graduated from 8 x 6 feet to 12 x 6 feet!

It was decided that Raymond should train for ordination as an Anglican priest at Coates Hall, the theological college of the Scottish Episcopal Church in Edinburgh, while continuing to reside with the community at Roslyn. At the same time, he worked on his thesis on Thomas Merton.[23] He was supervised by Brother Roland, with whom he would empathise for he, too, was a person of learning, possessed with an extraordinary ability to communicate matters of faith.[24] It is presumed that he stayed here until his ordination to the diaconate and subsequently to the priesthood in 1972 in St Mary's Cathedral, Glasgow. Brother James Halsey remembers him as a larger-than-life character, supremely gifted spiritually, intellectually and practically.

Ramon recalls in *The Prayer Mountain* his call to the ministry:

> It was four o'clock in the morning, when I was 21 years old. I was on night duty at Sully Hospital on the Glamorgan coast. The full moon shone on the still sea, and from my third-storey ward it reflected in calm serenity upon the water.
>
> At that very moment I felt it: an interior call that said, 'You must serve Me in the Church of God.' There was no question about it. Immediately before writing the night report, I penned a letter setting the wheels in motion towards training for ordination. The time had come.[25]

The year that he spent at Roslyn was crucial, for it was here that those seeds which were to germinate, grow and flourish in his exploration of the contemplative life were first sown. Here he gave himself wholeheartedly to the discipline of prayer and community life. The monk, Thomas Merton, was obviously an important influence on him. He refers to him in his introduction to his book, *Soul Friends* as 'one of the small band of loving soul-friends who regularly pray for me within the communion of saints'.[26] Like Merton, he prided himself on his broad view of Christianity: 'Merton's understanding of the gospel is both Evangelical and Catholic, and the incarnate Christ is the One who, as cosmic mediator, carries the believer, the church and the world into the experience of the universal mystery of love.'[27] These are themes which constantly occur in Ramon's writings.

Of Merton he says: 'In him I found a man who not only allowed the Spirit to free him from early rigid dogmatism, but who actually undertook a pilgrimage which involved body, mind and spirit.'[28] *Soul Friends* gives us a helpful insight into the spirituality of Merton. Comparison of the two may be unhelpful, but the attractiveness of both personalities is something that cannot lightly be dismissed. Merton lived a solitary life in a hut in the grounds of the monastery. But was it a solitary existence? It is apparent that he didn't cut himself off from his brothers. He shared meals with them and appeared daily at the monastery to collect his mail. Ramon, on the other hand, was extremely strict about this. While at Hilfield and Tymawr, living out the hermit life, he kept away from all contacts with other people and it was only latterly when he had settled at Glasshampton that he occasionally allowed a visit from friends or those who needed his counsel and advice. (I recall being on retreat at Tymawr, well aware that my friend was just a few fields away, but knowing that I should respect his need for privacy to lead a true hermit life. So during that week we never met!)

Merton sought to share his thoughts on the contemplative life with his readers and in this there appears to be a dichotomy. One of his biographers says of him:

Merton comes very close to an 'elitist' view of the contemplative life. For while he believed that God manifests himself in all who love him, he seemed to feel that the solitude and discipline essential to contemplation simply could not be achieved 'in the world'. People who live in the world and unite themselves to God 'in the activities of their lives' may very well have an extremely simple prayer life that brings them to 'the threshold of contemplation'. But it is difficult, if not very nearly impossible, for them to cross the threshold into the realms of true contemplation.[29]

Yet, in many of his books, he invites his readers to share in the contemplative experience. For example, this is one recommendation he gives to 'help the harassed layman to take his first steps on the path to a kind of contemplation':

Active virtue and good works play a large part in the 'contemplative' life that is led in the world, and the uncloistered man of prayer is most likely to be what we have called a 'masked contemplative'.[30]

Ramon is far more definite: contemplation is for everyone. The 'cell' is not reserved for monks or hermits; the cell is deep within the heart of every person and in it Christ dwells. In *A Month with Saint Francis,* he quotes one of Francis' sayings:

Wherever we are, wherever we go, we bring our cell with us. Our brother body is our cell and our soul is the hermit living in the cell, in order to pray to God and meditate. If our soul does not live in peace and solitude within its cell, of what avail is it to live in a man-made cell?[31]

In the years that follow, we see this whole idea becoming a reality as the hermit life is explored and Ramon finds his vocation in the solitude and silence where God is and where he has communion with him in that cell which is deep within.

The Franciscan

A revival of the Religious Life in the Church of England began in the mid-1880s. In 1905, the Anglican community of St Francis was inaugurated by a group of sisters in Hull, while in 1921, under the leadership of Brother Douglas (Douglas Downes), the brotherhood of St Francis was born. The brothers made their home at Flowers Farm at Batcombe in Dorset, close to Cerne Abbas. Later, the house and the surrounding land became known as Hilfield Friary. Here, the brothers combined both preaching and teaching with a simple life founded on the principles of St Francis, which included prayer, meditation, work on the land and the rehabilitation of homeless men ('wayfarers' as they were then known). In the 1960s, both the brothers' and sisters' communities expanded with a considerable growth in the numbers of those joining. This resulted in the foundation of new houses in Cambridge, Plaistow, Stepney, Alnmouth and Llandudno, where the saintly Brother Silyn Roberts, an ardent Welshman, was in charge. At the same time, the monastery at Glasshampton, near Worcester, became a place of prayer and study as well as a centre for novice formation.

Ramon settled at Hilfield, where he was clothed as a novice of SSF on 20 December 1978. With his entry into the Franciscan community came a change of name. He chose the name 'Ramon' after Raymond Lull (c. 1232–1315), a native of Spain and a Franciscan tertiary who, after years in solitude and study, became a missionary to the Muslims, suffering martyrdom at the age of 82 in his home country. He was beatified by Pope Pius IX in 1857. In a letter to Ron Powell, Ramon reflects on his new status:

> I feel it is an immense privilege to be in the habit and in the society, though there continues to be that restlessness about my perspective and understanding of life that will, I'm sure,

continue with me throughout my life. I have recently begun to think about it much more in terms of the old Welsh (indeed the whole Celtic) monastic pattern. St David would go off in his coracle to some lonely place or island and be alone with God in prayer, and then when the Spirit moved him he would go off and preach and teach with great fervour. It was a peripatetic life and ministry. I only hope that SSF will be able to put up with this kind of individualism.[32]

He made his first Profession three years later on Saturday 19 December 1981 at the friary before Brother Anselm, who was then the Provincial Minister. His announcement of this important event is written on a card in his own beautiful calligraphy, to which he adds these words of Thomas of Celano on St Francis:

Jesus he bore in his heart,
Jesus in his mouth,
Jesus in his ears,
Jesus in his eyes,
Jesus in the rest of his members…

Immediately on his arrival at the friary, Ramon threw himself into a busy life bordering on the hectic. His gifts were instantly recognised, for he was known as one who was 'good at everything' from gardening to cooking (see his menus for vegetarians in *The Listening Heart*), bookbinding, carpentry, painting, sewing (he made the habits for the brethren), sandal-making, poetry, writing, calligraphy and, of course, preaching and teaching. He soon found himself in demand as a retreat conductor. Among his first engagements was a retreat day for clergy and ministers of several denominations at Boscombe near Bournemouth. As usual, he hitchhiked to his destination, which gave him the opportunity to meet a variety of people whose company he enjoyed. He came to see this as part of his ministry. The brown-habited figure with thumb outstretched did not have to wait long before a car or lorry would draw up.

The stories he told of his adventures while travelling are numerous. He was once given a lift by a lorry driver who had financial difficulties, which had weighed on him to the extent that he had acute depression. Ramon listened to him and counselled him and finally prayed with him. A year later, the man's wife stopped to give a lift to a Franciscan, recognising his brown habit. She told him that she never stopped to give lifts to people, but she did on this occasion as the previous year another Franciscan had helped her husband to recover from his depressive state. She did not realise that this was the very person and was so delighted when she found out that she took him back to her house so that he could meet again her new, changed husband.

On his way to Boscombe to conduct the retreat, a car halted and he met the passengers – three young people, two men and a young woman, all of whose marriages had broken up. They had just visited the woman's former husband in Dorchester Prison. The woman told him that she never went to church but that she often read the Bible and prayed, and that started what must have been a very interesting and lively conversation! The retreat day on Thomas Merton was held at The House of Bethany Convent, which was situated in picturesque grounds. In the depths of an icy winter, he marvelled at its setting and said, 'The last talk was on prayer and the created order and the setting was so wonderful for it.'

The retreat at Boscombe led to a further invitation to meet with a larger group of young adults at a Methodist House. There, again, he talked about prayer as it applied to people attempting to live out the Christian faith in a secular world. Thus began a round of visits to various churches, groups and organisations where he met with folk who soon responded enthusiastically to what he had to say and were challenged as they made their faith journey.

On the practical side, in the friary, he worked for a while in the garden before his talents as a painter and decorator were discovered. He loved painting and threw himself into the task of redecorating St Clare's

Chapel where the Blessed Sacrament was reserved, before turning to paint the Recreation Room and the Refectory. In between, he was committed to joining the brothers in the chapel for the Daily Office, the Eucharist and sharing in the rhythm of prayer and meditation in the early hours of each day. He was then invited by the Guardian, Brother Bernard, to work in the office where his administrative skills were put to good use and where he was able to gain a bird's-eye view of the movements of the brothers and the ongoing work of the society, not only in this country but in other parts of the world.

In these early days, he recalls one particular Sunday when Brother John Francis took him to visit the *Carceri* or Hermitage which was well hidden in a forest above the friary. He was enraptured by the scene that greeted him and describes it:

> What a place! Even I was speechless! It is a beautiful, modest wooden structure with two levels. The door level consists of one cell with a small fireplace, a kitchen corner, working surfaces and a bed, and the lower level is still above ground because of the steep slope on which it is situated – this lower level is a chapel. It is so ideal for getting away from the busy friary, and I shall certainly make use of it for prayer, preparation of talks, retreats, etc. and for the preparation of some of the lectures which I am now beginning to give within the Society. I am now preparing a series of lectures on 'The Atonement'.[33]

One Sunday, he celebrated the Eucharist and preached at a little church about ten miles away from Hilfield where a number of children were present. He was in his element and told them a story instead of preaching a sermon. One little girl said, 'I wish I had brought my new dressing gown with a hood, then I would have been like you!' Compline at the friary was at 9.30 pm, which traditionally marked the end or 'completion' of the day's activities – but not for Ramon: 'After Compline I had to dress someone's wounds, examine and treat a wayfarer's terribly swollen and blistered feet, and then get off to bed. Life is quite varied.'

His novitiate was indeed a busy time. But deep under the surface was a persistent longing for solitude and the contemplative life. It was this that led him to discuss with the Guardian of the friary and his spiritual director the possibility of being excused all engagements for a period of six months in order to pursue an experiment in silence and solitude. Permission was granted. The next step was to seek out a suitable place for this to happen. He was not averse to spending this period in the grounds of Hilfield, provided that he was out of earshot of the friary and out of sight of its visitors and guests. The Guardian assisted him in the search and it was not long before they discovered the ideal spot in a wooded secluded area. A small wooden hut was purchased. One of the handymen who worked at the friary helped to install some insulation, fit some shelves, a bed and a desk and a gas camping stove to meet his cooking requirements. A rather precarious lean-to housed an Elsan toilet. In this hut in a remote corner of the Hilfield grounds, he would spend six months from 17 March to 17 September. Shortly before the venture began, he wrote a letter to his many friends outlining his proposal with a gentle warning that during this period there would be no letters.

> Prayer is the primary thing, saturated with scripture. There will be times of study, writing, manual work, etc., but the important thing will be that I am just 'there', open to God, and since I believe that it is he who has drawn me there, then the initiative must be with him as to the reason for my being there. I have a very firm framework of liturgical prayer, study, manual work, and a big patch of garden for vegetables – but any or all of this can be laid aside for the sake of silence and prayer.

> I shall be remembering you especially at the Eucharist and during the whole of Sunday morning prayer, so perhaps you will remember me especially as you go to worship on the Lord's Day.[34]

So, on St Patrick's Day in 1982, he left the community chapel accompanied by Brother Bernard for the enclosed area. His new home was blessed with incense and holy water, the Eucharist was celebrated and, after he had said 'goodbye' to the brethren and the outside world, he began the process of settling down to a new way of life. During the months that followed, he was completely undisturbed except for three official visits from the Provincial Minister and the Guardian. In fact, no one discovered where he was! It was here that the pattern was set for the future occasions when he was to live as a hermit. His day lasted from 4.00 am to 8.30 pm and his time was divided in this way:

4.30 am	Night office
5.15 am	Jogging
6.30 am	Ablutions and breakfast
8.00 am	Matins and meditation
9.00 am	Study and prayer
12.00	Midday office (Eucharist on Holy Days)
1.00 pm	Main meal
2.00 pm	Manual work (garden, bookbinding, painting, etc.)
5.00 pm	Evensong and meditation
6.00 pm	Light supper, followed by reading/study/writing/prayer
8.30 pm	Compline and bed

He made an allowance for some variation in this pattern, sometimes transferring manual work to the early morning and, when he felt the need, spending more time in prayer. From sunset on Thursday until sunset on Friday he fasted, and on Sundays after the Eucharist he would, as he had promised his friends, spend the morning in intercessory prayer going through some 500 people on his list, believing this to be an important dimension of his ministry.

Six months later, he emerged from solitude and silence to be reunited with the brothers in the friary. Reflecting on this experience, Ramon remembers it as a time of great joy when that longing in his heart for love and prayer leading to a deeper relationship with God became a reality. He admits in one of his letters that the times of intense joy were accompanied by some darkness, conflict and a little bit of *accidie* in between.[35] But this period confirmed his desire for a more contemplative lifestyle.

> I see the vocation of the solitary and hermit (or whatever you call one who is drawn to prayer in solitude), not as a cabbage-growing lover of nature who finds human contact not amenable, but one who obeys the inward prompting of the divine Spirit to prayer and intercession; one united in Christ's passion and sufferings, sharing already in the glory and victory of the resurrection, and girded with the armour of God in conflict with the powers of darkness for the redemption of the world and the manifestation of Christ in glory.[36]

The seeds that were sown in the Hermits' Symposium were now beginning to take root, for he says of this period:

> Solitude is the context of my inward search – and I *must* continue for I cannot live without that Love which I have only glimpsed, but glimpsing causes me to long for it.[37]

The following year (1983) saw Ramon back in circulation meeting deadlines for the books he continued to write, speaking and preaching, training novices and leading missions at the Anglican and United Reformed Churches in Bracknell, then at Ketton in Lincolnshire and later as the Franciscan missioner at Keble College, Oxford as part of the university mission. After conducting a retreat for the Othona Community in Dorset, October saw him taking part in a month's mission in the diocese of Swansea and Brecon at the invitation of the bishop, Rt Revd B.N.Y. Vaughan. This was to be his last 'big' event. Together with a team of six, which included Brother Silyn SSF and Father Aidan Mayoss of the Community of the Resurrection, he travelled the length and breadth of the diocese, which extends from Rhosili at the southern end of the Gower Peninsula to the northern hills of Radnorshire. The theme was to be 'The Trinity' and, as part of the preparation for this event, the missioners were invited to play a prominent part in the Diocesan

Clergy School, which met at the University at Lampeter earlier in the year. In his opening address, Ramon, as leader of the team, eloquently, energetically and full of his usual enthusiasm reflected on his personal experience of God as Trinity, particularly with reference to his conversion. He spoke of his knowledge as a child of God as Father, in spite of the fact that he was brought up in a non-churchgoing home. He then referred to his conversion to Christ at the age of 12 and his subsequent receiving of the Holy Spirit at the age of 16. The lecture, however, was not well received by many of the clergy. For them it was simplistic, over-personalised, subjective, unacademic, lacking in theological content and not what they had expected from the leading speaker at the conference and one who had been chosen to head up the forthcoming mission.

The questions betrayed some disappointment and concern about the content of the future diocesan mission event. However, in his humble and gentle way Ramon accepted the criticism and the following day produced a lecture which was to allay the fears of all who were present. This second address produced a totally different reaction. He proceeded to demonstrate his vast knowledge as a theologian and Christian apologist (described by one of the clergy as 'mind-blowing'). Ramon was steeped in biblical knowledge; he had studied the teachings of the early Fathers and was able to quote freely from contemporary theologians and commentators. As a result, the critics readily retracted their former criticism, recognising that they were listening to a scholar who knew what he was talking about. The effect was quite revealing. Ramon did not retract anything he had said in the first lecture. He proceeded to describe the classic Trinitarian teaching with a background of wide reading and study, showing that for him academic theology was equally as important as personal experience:

Classic Trinitarian teaching says that each person of the Holy Trinity participates in the life and action of the others; there is a holy interpenetration of being and love. From this, I understand that God (Father, Son and Holy Spirit) was at work in his fullness from my earliest days: so the Son and the Spirit were active in my early intuitive understanding of the divine, mysterious presence in the cosmos; the Father and the Spirit were at work in my evangelical conversion; and the Father and the Son were manifest in the experience of release which I identified with my baptism in the Holy Spirit...

My understanding of God is an experiential one, a biblical one, but a dynamic one. The Father loves the Son... loves the Spirit... loves the Father... And within the Body of Christ I am drawn into an experienced participation: the historic work of redemption and reconciliation which Christ effected is cosmic in its scope, and will be manifested in the whole created order.[38]

Over the month of October, mission services were held each week at four centres (Brecon Cathedral, Holy Trinity in Llandrindod Wells, St David's Morriston and St Paul's Sketty) at which each member of the team took it in turns to give an address. The days between were spent visiting parishes, speaking to groups, meeting children in schools and encouraging the clergy. From this frenzied activity Ramon, together with Brother Silyn, returned to Glasshampton before travelling to North Wales to finalise his plans for a further period of hermit life.

The month-long mission brought an end to Ramon's preaching ministry with one exception. Every year in the summer, he travelled to Swansea to visit his sister, her family and his many friends, and on one Sunday of his annual leave he would always preach at St James' Swansea. He was an outstanding preacher, holding the attention of his listeners throughout his sermons, which were often quite long. Their eyes would be riveted on him as he expounded the Sunday readings, using stories and illustrations. His language was simple. His message was direct and relevant. Words seem to pour out from his lips. No wonder my parishioners looked forward to his annual visit. I once complimented him on his sermon and he replied, 'Well, Arthur, you have to preach every Sunday of the year. I only have to preach once!' Brother Austin remembers one occasion when he was serving at a Eucharist at which Ramon was presiding and preaching. He noticed that the sermon had nothing to do with his postcard notes. 'When I questioned him, he replied, "I decided that what I'd planned was wrong for those who were here, so I did another."'

Sadly, a few days after the diocesan mission, Brother Silyn died at Glasshampton. Ramon said that it was as Silyn would wish. He would have preferred to die after hard work than to rust away at the end of his life.

On the Lleyn

Jutting out to sea in North West Wales lies the Lleyn Peninsula, with its sandy beaches attracting today's tourists. It was once the much-travelled route for pilgrims to Bardsey, a famous place for pilgrimage in medieval times. Their journey would take them through Clynnog Fawr, where St Beuno established his monastery, on to Pistyll, with its seventh-century church and hospice where tired pilgrims would rest before continuing to Aberdaron at the furthest tip of the peninsular. Here, they would stock up with food before making the crossing to Bardsey Island, their destination. Bardsey is known in Welsh as Ynys Elli, 'The Island of Tides'. Aptly named, the island has dangerous currents which often mean that the crossing is impossible. In Celtic lands, monastic life was lived out on remote islands like this off the coasts of Wales and Ireland, places which were isolated and distant from the 'world'.

These islands were the equivalent of those desert places in Egypt which attracted people like Anthony and Athanasius to a movement which began at the end of the third century. Here, these Desert Fathers and Mothers sought isolation from the distractions of society in order to follow the example of Jesus in the wilderness. They took literally the words which Jesus spoke to the rich young man: 'If you would be perfect, go, sell what you possess and give to the poor, and you will have treasure in heaven; and come, follow me' (Matthew 19:21, ESV). These were their marching orders and the way of life which evolved was designed to enable them to accept the challenge to forsake the world and dedicate themselves unreservedly to following Jesus. As he had withdrawn to the desert to commune with his Father, so for them the goal was union with God through prayer, meditation and contemplation. By the fourth century, the deserts on the periphery of the western edge of the Nile Delta and the wilderness of Judea witnessed several clusters of such communities practicing strict fasting while disciplining the body and mind in this life of complete dedication. Subsequently, this movement was to influence Welsh monasticism in the fifth and sixth centuries. The community at Bardsey was founded by St Cadfan, who sailed with Padarn and a few monks from Brittany and landed at Tywyn, where he and his followers settled beside a spring near the seashore. From there, he went on to establish his community at Bardsey.

In the ninth and tenth centuries, the island suffered as a result of Viking invasion but, when peace was established, it became a place of significance in Welsh religious history, attracting so many pilgrims to its shores that it was known as the 'Rome of Britain'. Ramon was familiar with Bardsey, where he had on occasion spent some time as a chaplain to its pilgrims and tourists in the summer months. He was attracted to the island, to its isolation and long tradition as a place of holiness, pilgrimage and retreat. He had discussed the possibility of settling there as a hermit, but the community was aware of the dangers of seclusion on such an inaccessible and remote island and refused to grant him permission to live there. Consequently, it was on the mainland on the opposite coast at Mynydd Anelog that Ramon found what he was looking for – a small, hundred-year-old cottage tucked away from the road with a glorious view of the nearby island. The cottage was owned by a farmer who was a friend of the Provincial Minister. During the summer months he rented it out, but it was unoccupied in the winter because of its bleakness and distance from civilisation. Visitors here would also have to cope with the strong gales blowing in from the Irish Sea. Looking across the island and aware of the history of Bardsey, traditionally known as the island of 20,000 saints, Ramon would be reminded of the 'thin veil' which separated earth from heaven and would rejoice in the fellowship of those saints who had trod this path before him. He would have taken note of the warning of his spiritual director that he was in for a hard time and that the winter season, with dark nights, winds and a storm-tossed sea, would inevitably have their effect on him.

Canon Donald Allchin, one of Ramon's spiritual directors and a former canon of Canterbury Cathedral, immersed himself in the Welsh spiritual tradition and, towards the end of his life, was Professor of Welsh and Theology at Bangor University. In his article in *Boundless Grandeur,* Dr Patrick Thomas reflects on Allchin's love of Bardsey:

> As he reflected on Enlli's long tradition with the monastic tradition, both in the pre-Norman 'Age of Saints' and in the medieval period, Donald saw these centuries of prayer as having had a transforming influence on the island. To his mind, it had become a place where there was neither past nor future – only the present moment as a moment of eternity. He commented that on Enlli phrases like 'the communion of saints' and 'the cloud of witnesses' take on a new significance for us. We are 'with angels and archangels and with the whole company of heaven'.[39]

Within St Hywyn's Church, the parish church of Aberdaron, the furthest point of the promontory overlooking Bardsey, there are two gravestones from the fifth and sixth centuries thought to be the final resting place of two monks. The stones were found at the foot of Mynydd Anelog, close to Ramon's cottage. The inscription records the burial of 'Seneca, the Priest, together with many brethren'. Andrew Jones, Archdeacon of Meirionydd, and an experienced leader of pilgrimages, in his book *Pilgrimage,* says of Bardsey:

> One of the comments I hear most often from pilgrims is that the accumulated prayer over the centuries on the island is almost tangible. Certainly the place gives itself freely and abundantly to those who seek to pray, and there are many spots that provide space to do this: a chapel, a ruined abbey, an oratory, a well, cliff edges, beaches, mountain top, open spaces and hidden niches here and there. They all invite us to join in the prayers of those Christian pilgrims who have sought God here for almost 1,500 years and to join in what we might think of

as the island's own prayer – the wordless, indefinable (yet somehow real) link between creation and Creator.[40]

Inevitably, as Anelog was on the pilgrim route, that atmosphere would have overflowed on to the mainland from where Ramon could view the island in all weathers. His report to Sister Mary Clare,[41] his spiritual director, reflects some of his first reactions to this new world:

> I do not know what the outcome will be – I already see that the golden sunshine and quiet beauty of a Dorset summer in green woodland is past, and the winter among the cliffs and rocks of the Lleyn Peninsula with the heave and swell of the restless sea has caught me already in its mood. As I write, darkness and mist fall over the mountain, the cry of the high wind echoes around the cottage and the dim outlines of the surrounding rocky heights bear witness to the austerity of the months to come. But the mystic fire burns within, and the longing for the Beloved and the pain of absence mingle in the way that opens before me.[42]

Ramon had spoken excitedly about his proposed experiment in hermit living at the Lampeter conference for the clergy of the diocese of Swansea and Brecon in the previous July. It was shortly after the subsequent mission in October 1983 that he began the adventure. His exuberance and enthusiasm were infectious, and it was difficult for us to imagine that one who was so gregarious and outgoing, with a passion for communicating the gospel to people, should want to spend six months in complete isolation and silence in such an inhospitable place, particularly in the winter months. But the decision had been made. In a car packed with foodstuffs contributed by neighbouring parishes, where he had preached and explained to congregations why he was making this move, all was ready for the journey to North Wales. On his return to Hilfield, he was to write:

> I want to say how grateful I am to those who not only prayed for me throughout the time (and this was the primary thing),

but also gave me edible and other gifts so that there was no fear of me starving to death! The great kindness of the parishes around the friary, and friends of SSF was manifest in most concrete ways. I packed our vehicle with tins of coffee, dried milk, beans, spaghetti, rice, fruit, tomatoes, Christmas cake, preserved fruit, jams, marmalade, dried fruit, lentils, beans of all varieties (soya, mung, field, blackeye, haricot, butter and kidney!). My vegetarian diet was rich in protein of right combinations, and I remain as healthy as ever – an important factor in living alone.[43]

At the cottage, Ramon practised the routine he had established at his first experiment in hermit living at Hilfield the previous year (see 'The Franciscan' on page 39). Some days, he would observe walkers making their way up the nearby path peering over the wall to see who this lonely person might be. His day began in the darkness before the dawn and was punctuated by the Daily Office – prayers, the recitation of psalms and readings – periods of prayer and meditation and, on Sundays, the Eucharist followed, as at Hilfield, by intercession for some 500 people, many of whom had asked him to pray for them. In addition to his spiritual exercises, he also made room for physical exercise, well aware of the necessity of keeping a healthy body. He was strict about his vegetarian diet, carefully ensuring that this was well-balanced and nutritious. He discovered that the plentiful supply of dry heather which surrounded him on the hillside provided effective kindling when rarely he succumbed to the luxury of lighting a fire in the hearth, sometimes a necessity in the dark, cold nights that followed. There were periods of reading, study and work. He would tend his garden and enjoy walks along the cliff paths while playing his recorder. He always regretted that he had not had music lessons, for he loved to sing and had a beautiful singing voice.

Reading his letters and extracts from his journal, we are left in no doubt that there were times when he was overcome by spiritual darkness[44] – occasionally, more conscious of the absence of God than his presence. This does not surprise us as we imagine the effect his surroundings must have had on him (as Donald Allchin had foretold) – the darkness enfolding him, the howling wind (often at gale force), the heavy rainfall and the storm-tossed sea below.

In his books, he reminds us of his own experiences of God. These are recorded with humility and as a means of encouragement to us, his readers, as we make our journey through life. He recalls an event at Anelog on a winter's day in Advent, an experience which really shook him. It happened on a bleak and menacing day, a dark day physically and spiritually. It was mid-December and he had not seen a living soul since he had arrived the previous month. He didn't expect to see anyone until February, when it was arranged for the Guardian to visit him. Suddenly, he was aware of the loneliness of the place. It seemed to descend upon him. It was painful and it was a completely new experience which he had never felt before. As the daylight gave way to darkness, a gloom and bleakness seemed to penetrate into his heart and mind. He felt desperately the need for company and then quite suddenly there was a knocking at the door and miraculously there standing on the threshold in overcoat, beret and wellington boots was Father Donald Allchin who, while visiting two hermits in the area, thought he might see if Ramon was all right. It couldn't have been a better time for a visit, for Ramon was at the end of his tether. He describes the visit:

> 'Oh Donald,' I said, 'I'm amazed and so pleased to see you today.' I was overwhelmed by the Lord's timing, and especially in the light of his first words: 'Didn't you receive my letter? I wrote to you about two weeks ago.' I collected my sparse mail from the back of a farmhouse at the bottom of Anelog on Friday mornings, and Father Allchin's letter arrived a few days later, on 18 December!
>
> We were soon sitting together sharing what I had written, for he was the very man I needed at that time in that place for that particular need. He understood perfectly where I was at that time, and what my needs were. He had himself a similar

experience of being strangely and simply taken into the Lord's will.[45]

Looking back, he values those periods of silence and calm when he was able to glorify God for the staggering beauty of the world around him.

> I am not unaware of the severity, the darkness, the grief, the pain that I have stored within me. There are hours of days of silent weeping still; there is the aching love and loneliness and longing. But there is also, because of this, the awareness of the divine Love, the mystery of the dark night and the path of purgation leading to illumination and union with God. I am becoming aware of the unity of the whole pattern, of the interweave of human love and grief, and of the fact that not one thread will be missing, and that the warp and woof of his weaving will bring me to death and to life. It is not a way I could have chosen, though I see that I have chosen it; it is not a way I could desire, though I do desire it more than all; it is not a way I can take, for I am afraid – but I do take it with courage and strength and fear and glory.[46]

> One of the most precious experiences of the time was to descend into the depths beyond my own individuality into a profound corporate sense of our common humanity with its pains and joys, and to find that the divine Love is in and through all, and will ultimately be manifested as 'all in all'.[47]

As spring gave way to summer, Ramon's retreat to Anelog was swiftly drawing to a close. The six months was up. It had, as he admitted, been a time of mixed moods with ups and downs, but it was undoubtedly a revealing experience which did not discourage him. In his journal he wrote:

> I am preparing to leave this place with a certain sorrow and an immense sense of gratitude. The few people who know what

the life of prayer in solitude is about forecast that the second period would not be the 'honeymoon' experience of light and glory as was much of the former Dorset period, but they assure me of their prayers and the rightness of the way… As well as times of darkness and helplessness, there have been periods of interior joy and a deeper understanding of my part in the mystery of salvation, as a man, as a friar, as part of the Body of Christ.[48]

He returned to Glasshampton, where for seven years he continued to share the routine of the Franciscan life of prayer and work while teaching the novices and writing books. For some years he was Guardian at the monastery, where the tradition of welcome and hospitality continued to be practised. A regular but disturbed visitor on one occasion set fire to the building. Fortunately, no great damage was done. The Fire Service reported the incident to the police, who in turn visited Glasshampton in order to have consent to prosecute the offender. Much to their surprise Ramon, as Guardian, refused. The officer pointed out that the man concerned was exploiting the monastery. Ramon's unanswerable retort was, 'We are here to be exploited, if necessary.'

In one of the letters he wrote from the Lleyn, he says:

It seems to me that whereas I swam out of the SSF harbour and was carried out with the current of apostolic work and evangelism with a quiet undercurrent of prayer, now the undercurrent has become the main pull and I am more and more unable to do the preaching/mission part.[49]

What began at a small hut in the grounds of Hilfield was continued, and the vocation to the hermit life was confirmed at Anelog. Ramon was soon ready for the next step in his journey, which was to take him to South Wales; this time to a caravan in a field close to Tymawr Convent.

The Tymawr years

In 1909 a new vicar, Revd Dr Ernest Glover, arrived in the parish of Rumboldswyke in the diocese of Chichester. He soon became aware of a group of ladies in the parish who were trying to lead a life of prayer and service. From this small group emerged a nucleus that was prepared to dedicate themselves to life in community. Eventually, a villa was purchased in Lyndurst Road, Chichester (where one room became an oratory) and the Society of the Sacred Cross was born.[50] By 1920, the Chichester house had become inadequate for the needs of a growing community of sisters and the owner of the house wanted to sell it. In November of that year, a house in Monmouth was advertised in the *Church Times*. The sisters looked at it and immediately saw that it was just what they wanted. The property was purchased and this became the new home of the Society in January 1923. The house, Tymawr, was situated in the hills above the River Wye close to the ruined Cistercian abbey at Tintern where the silent life (which is so much part of the character of Tymawr) had been practised for many centuries. In beautiful surroundings, Tymawr Convent has witnessed throughout its existence in the Benedictine contemplative tradition, where daily prayer and worship continue to be offered and where retreatants are welcomed. The society owned much of the surrounding land and it was in a plum orchard some distance from the house that Ramon lived in a caravan for three years.

This three-berth caravan had been advertised for sale in a local newspaper in Worcester. It seemed to be just what he was looking for, so with Brother Amos and his friend, Mervyn, a journey was made to Stourport where a couple sold it to him for £350. It was soon paid for by some well-wishers. Curtains were made, some foam cushions were provided, a worktop fitted and some awning to provide extra sheltered space was waterproofed. Early in August 1990, the hermitage caravan was towed from Glasshampton

Monastery to Tymawr Convent. At the end of the month, after receiving Communion at the convent chapel, a small group including Brother Amos, Mother Gillian and Father James Coutts made its way to the plum orchard where the caravan was now in place and ready to be occupied. It was sprinkled with holy water, Psalm 122 and some prayers were said and Ramon moved into his new home. On 2 September, just a few days after his arrival, he wrote in his journal:

> Over the last few days, I have lain low and feel something like a death has taken place and is still taking place in me. I am only now realising that I have cut myself off from all my friends and am in a very precarious psychological state. And for the first time I wonder if I will be able to make it through the first year... I look forward to seeing Father Donald on 23 September.[51]

In the early days at Tymawr, the sisters had a full complement of members (25+) with the result that the menial tasks were easily shared. They tended the extensive grounds, cut the grass, gathered in the hay, cultivated flowers, fruit and vegetables, made bread, fed their cattle and poultry and operated a small printing press while also managing to keep the premises in good repair. However, as numbers declined, such a workload was both unpractical and impossible if they were to maintain the true purpose of their life – the *Opus Dei*. Subsequently, the livestock was sold, much of the surrounding land rented to a neighbouring farmer while some of the manual work was handed over to a willing band of volunteers. A strong, able pair of hands belonging to a Franciscan friar was most welcome and Ramon was delighted to have this opportunity of giving something back to the community in return for the hospitality he received. His caravan was conveniently situated in an isolated spot a few fields away from the convent. In the early hours of each morning, when the sisters were engaged in the chapel, he would perform his daily tasks – watering and feeding the poultry, gardening, chopping wood, painting and decorating and, where needed, doing maintenance jobs. When his work was completed, it was back to the caravan for ablutions, the morning office and a period of meditation. Every day began with this pattern, except for Sunday when he would celebrate the Eucharist and spend a long time fulfilling his promise to intercede for people on his prayer list. Knowing the dangers of a sedentary life, he would make sure that there was room for physical exercise as part of the daily rhythm. So, he would spend an hour jogging or cycling along the nearby lanes, breathing the fresh air of the quiet countryside and drinking the fresh waters of its beauty. This, after all, was God's creation and it mirrored the unutterable beauty of his glory.

Ramon had always lived a frugal, simple life. Friends in Scotland said that he arrived there with practically nothing and went away with nothing! Life in the caravan was certainly frugal with just the bare necessities for his survival. He had a small gas cooker fuelled by a 15 kg butane gas cylinder. The cooker had two rings, a grill and an oven for him to bake his bread. In Lleyn, he had spent the winter with no heat and had planned to do the same at Tymawr. He had been presented with a two-wick paraffin lamp, which he planned to use when the nights got darker. His timetable provided room for such domestic chores as bread-making, washing his clothes, digging the loo in a nearby field and various other jobs. In the November following his arrival, the weather suddenly turned cold and wet and soon ice began to appear, but things were to become worse in the following month. Such was the intense cold that one morning the butane gas froze as well as the water inside the caravan. Then the storms came. In the nights, torrential rain would beat relentlessly on the caravan roof which, together with the wind, caused the canvas awning to billow dangerously. In spite of his efforts to re-anchor it, when the gales reached between 70 and 80 mph, the supports finally collapsed. The damage was irreparable and he knew that from then on he would have to manage without it. This presented him with a problem, for the awning had provided shelter for supplies for which there was not room to store indoors.

His diet was simple, too. In *Heaven and Earth,* he provides a few examples of his dishes. There is a variety of concoctions which are combined with various beans, pulses, pasta, rice, TVP (textured vegetable protein) mince, Sosmix, nut-roast or hard-boiled eggs. Breakfast was a bowl of porridge, while he would have a bread roll with honey, jam or marmalade in the evening.

He soon settled down to the same strict routine he had kept at Anelog. In a letter to his friend, Ron, on the last day of 1990, he admitted that he missed people but did not feel lonely. His aloneness, he says, 'casts me back to the Lord who seems to have called me to this place at this time for his own purposes – and his purposes are always purposes of love'.[52]

The following year, among the letters he received was one from Connecticut, where the Society of St John the Evangelist, a Benedictine Anglican Order with its mother house at Cowley in Oxford, had a monastery. It was a request asking him to conduct a community retreat the following June. Inevitably, he declined what must have been an attractive invitation, aware that he had said 'goodbye' to lecturing and preaching, the kind of ministry he felt was no longer meant for him.

In another letter, he says that he has relaxed his rule a bit and was prepared to meet with one or two people a month to share with them something of their spiritual journey. He emphasises that these visits are not 'social' but precious times to engage in the 'pilgrimage' of life in which all are involved. He also writes of an invitation he has received to continue his hermit life on Bardsey Island:

> That invitation, as you can imagine, was full of challenge and adventure – and the Island which would be cut off for the whole of the winter, with just two other people there, would have been a hermit's delight (with darker repercussions too, I'm sure). The strange thing is that I have not felt that interior affirmation that I look for in making such a decision. It seems to me that I have laid a good foundation here since 1990, and my roots have gone down so that fruit is now beginning to appear, and STABILITY

seems the right word from my point of view and as a witness to and from SSF. I don't want them to feel that I want to go hiving off after every new invitation that comes along.[53]

He also had plans to develop his hermitage by building a stone cell on to a derelict wall in the next field, which would mean laying a concrete floor, knocking three windows into the existing three walls, and building a wall/door/window into the fourth side. These plans, however, as we shall see, never materialised.

Although the small caravan in which he lived had been insulated, in its exposed position it could be extremely cold, particularly when it was buffeted by the winter wind. While he had made every effort to keep himself fit, these conditions were a test of anyone's robustness. Three days after Christmas in 1992, he awoke suddenly in the night with severe vertigo.

Everything swinging and swimming around me so that I had to grab hold of the edge of my bunk to avoid falling out, this together with hot and cold sweats, temperature and palpitations. This lasted up to 15 mins, then receded and went on intermittently through much of the night. I tried to get up at about 4.15 am but keeled over, then I found that if I knelt upright on my prayer stool the dizziness abated. All this, of course, in the darkness and solitude of fields around![54]

It is hard to imagine one of such great faith being frightened, but such symptoms must have caused him more than a little concern. After telling the sisters the following morning, he got to the local GP who diagnosed that the basic problem was soaring blood pressure. The doctor took blood samples and immediately put him on medication. Next day he had an appointment in Chepstow Hospital for a chest X-ray as the doctor suspected that there might be cardiac problems. However, the results were negative and proved that all was well as far as his heart was concerned. One consequence of this episode was that the doctor was far from happy with Ramon's accommodation.

Living outside in an unheated caravan in the depths of winter was asking for trouble, even for one who was proud of his good health and did everything to preserve it. As a temporary measure, he was offered a warm and cosy cell in the convent, but he felt that accepting this offer would be a sign of defeat. He explained to the doctor that this was not what he wanted, but promised that if the symptoms should return or his health deteriorated he would accept the sisters' hospitality. In spite of some dizzy spells, the symptoms lessened and his blood pressure returned to normal. This was a great relief to him, as he hated being ill and in fact had not seen a doctor for 20 years. The incident taught him many lessons:

> You can imagine 'me' in all this and how I have been knocked off my proud perch and learned so many lessons of weakness and dependence during these months. It has also affected concentration and manual work but I have found great help in the Jesus Prayer.[55]

This experience also confirmed that he had made the right decision regarding Bardsey. He now began to wonder how much longer he could stay at Tymawr and was already toying with the idea of following his vocation in a hut in the grounds of Glasshampton Monastery. Of one thing he was certain: that he could not spend another winter in a caravan without heat. Could converting the nearby barn into living quarters with a little heat be the answer? Apparently not.

By the summer of 1993, he had decided to move back to Glasshampton where he would live in two huts and continue to follow the hermit life in the shadow of the monastery. While sad at the prospect of leaving Tymawr, he believed that this was the right step. Arrangements were made for him to celebrate the Eucharist in the convent chapel on Sunday 29 August, exactly three years since his arrival. He planned to return to Glasshampton via Swansea, where he would be able to spend some time with Wendy, his sister, and her family and, as he had done for the past three years, preach at St James'. Before leaving the caravan, he gathered together all the correspondence he had received, together with carbon copies of his replies in plastic bags, to be destroyed. It was with some reluctance that he did this, realising that these letters told many precious stories of the pilgrimages of a variety of people from differing traditions. So ended another chapter. This is how he records the last days at Tymawr:

> I gave away my caravan, then gave up taking the medication which was making me feel very tired – I felt better without it! I'm still without it and the new GP says that we'll give it a trial without, and my throat is also improving! Anyway, I preached and celebrated the Eucharist for the SSC sisters... It was good and sad, but both realising the blessing the Lord had afforded us in being together in prayer and solitude, without any misunderstanding or negativity during the three years... I preached at St James', Swansea on the 12th – it was wonderful communicating again – tremendous feeling to have the congregation eating out of one's hand – dangerous, too, but so good if you have the word to preach! Then Gors School assembly and the classes on the Monday – it was good for me to feel that my communicative ability remains – and yet I know it is no longer the primary thing.[56]

Throughout the years, he continued to be in great demand as a spiritual writer. He loved writing, and his books reflect not only his strong conviction in matters of faith but a strong desire to help his readers on their faith journey, particularly in his teaching on prayer. He sent the royalties from his books to a donkey sanctuary in Dorset, as when he left Hilfield, Jacomena, the donkey he cared for, was eventually sent there as no brother was available to look after her and to give her the care she had previously received.

An avid reader, Ramon always had at least six books at hand: a children's book, a theological work, books on philosophy, a biography, German texts and crime fiction.

His books are full of quotations from writers he admired. A glance through the acknowledgement pages leaves us in no doubt that he read widely. He quotes from theologians like John Macquarrie, John Hick, J. Paterson Smyth, F.D. Maurice as well as traditional theologians like Clement of Alexandria, Origen and Julian of Norwich. The list is endless and fascinating. He also quotes from the writings of Buzz Aldrin, Terry Waite, Brian Keegan, Dietrich Bonhoeffer and Martin Israel. He was a great admirer of William Horwood, the author of *The Duncan Chronicle*. He wrote about a system of moles in which the STONE is the central symbol of mystery and holiness which guides and leads them in their personal and corporate lives. Of him he says, 'He is a Christian/Buddhist, and his books contain more theology and spirituality than many theological tomes.' The list is endless and demonstrates how well informed and knowledgeable he was.

The hermitage at Glasshampton

Glasshampton, an isolated estate some nine miles from Worcester, is situated in the parish of Astley and was once the site of a large mansion. Built in 1707, it had a chequered history. An engraving by Thomas Nash in his *History of Worcester* (1781) depicts the house as an imitation of a French chateau, with high imposing palisading on its front and approached by a long avenue of trees. Built by Sir Thomas Cookes, the house, on his death (as he had no children), became the property of a distant relative, Thomas Geers. Geers, like his benefactor, changed his name to Winford, who had been the squire at nearby Astley Manor.

Eventually, the property came into the hands of Revd D.J.J. Cooke, the wealthy curate of Astley. With ample means, he decided to rebuild the house entirely. The stables were added in 1809. In 1810, a fire broke out and the whole building, with the exception of the stable block, was completely destroyed. It was never rebuilt but the stable block, a fine building, was preserved and eventually became an Anglican monastery, due to the vision of Father William Sirr, a founder member of the Society of Divine Compassion. Father William was based in Plaistow in East London, where he and Father Andrew ministered to a population blighted by poverty and disease. In 1906, his picture appeared in the *Daily Mirror* under the headline: 'Clergy join procession of London's unemployed'. The article went on to report that 'Father William led the West Ham and Plaistow men with a banner with the words, "In the name of Christ we claim that all men should have the right to live."'

William had just been elected Superior of his community – a position he was to hold for the next six years. However, it was to the silent, solitary life of prayer that he was attracted, and in Glasshampton he found the ideal place for a house of prayer. He could see the potential of the stables. The owner, Mr Cecil Jones, responded positively to William's proposal, as did the community to which he owed allegiance. On 20 November 1918, he slept at Glasshampton for the first time. The building, approached from the main road by a rough lane, was in a state of disrepair and was barely habitable. For over a year, he proceeded energetically and single-handedly with a repair programme: salvaging wood, sweeping chimneys, building walls and lopping trees until eventually he was able to welcome visitors. This became his home and a home for those who for relatively short periods managed to endure not only the spartan accommodation in freezing conditions with a frugal diet, but also the strict spiritual discipline of the resident monk.

When he took up residence at Glasshampton, William was 57 years old and his hopes were that the community would grow quickly while he was still active and vigorous. Sadly, his dream failed to become a reality in his lifetime and he wrote in 1922:

We stand for something no other community stands for... quietness, hiddenness and simplicity. It *is* a difficult time... there have been so many disappointments. But, thank God, we are getting a few years of tradition behind us and after a few years of slow and steady progress we shall have won the confidence of a few. It is always difficult to go on with nothing to show.

For 18 years, Father William lived this lonely, stoical life. While many were attracted to his ideals and drew strength from the experience of sharing his life, what he had so eagerly and enthusiastically prayed for never happened. In the end, he reluctantly accepted: 'It is God's will, therefore it was the best thing that could have happened.' He died on Easter Day 1937 at a nursing home for clergy in Surrey.

The premises then had a chequered history. In the early years of World War II, the house was occupied by the Community of the Holy Cross, Haywards Heath, then by the Society of Friends until 1946, when it was taken over by the Society of St Francis as a house of retreat.

Glasshampton was well-known to Ramon. He had lived and worked there and served for some years as Guardian. In his mind, he had probably already planned where his hermitage should be situated: in an enclosure close to the monastery but far enough away from distractions. There he erected three small huts: one for his living quarters with the simplest of furnishings – a table with storage beneath, two chairs, a bed, a small stove and wash basin – and sufficient room to receive a steady stream of visitors (one at a time!). Alongside were the other huts – a small toilet and his workshop (10 x 6 feet), where he would spend some time most days doing practical work – bookbinding, sandal-making, mounting icons, constructing prayer stools and other tasks. A third hut served as his chapel. Here, above the small altar, hung a replica of the St Francis crucifix, the original hanging in the little church of St Damiano in Assisi. It was from this cross that Christ spoke to Francis. In this hut there was an atmosphere of peace and tranquillity where much prayer was offered. The enclosure was surrounded by trees and shrubs and a well-cared-for vegetable patch where he grew his own food. Overlooking a wooded area, St Peter's, Astley, where the hymn writer, Frances Ridley Havergal's father was once Rector,[57] could be seen in the distance.

To this site, after Evensong on St Francis' Day (4 October 1993), the brethren, equipped with incense and holy water, processed with Ramon from the monastery to bless the hermitage. Psalm 121 was said and prayers were offered 'that this place may manifest the mystery and glory of your love'. The Peace was shared and Ramon was left in his new home while the brothers made their way back to the house.

Ramon was by nature a happy person, full of joy, but it would not be an exaggeration to say that here in the hermitage at Glasshampton he was at his happiest. He would go to the nearby monastery for a shower and to raid the kitchen while the brothers were at Morning Prayer. Often, notes were left with small requests and information about visitors who were due. He continued to maintain a daily routine which differed little from that which he had already established at Anelog and Tymawr:

4.30 am	Contemplative prayer
6.30 am	Ablutions, breakfast, Morning Office
9.00 am	Morning work (garden, book binding, prayer stools/icon making)
12.30 pm	Midday prayer and main meal
2.30 pm	Afternoon work (study, writing, correspondence)
4.30 pm	Cup of tea, reading, Evening Prayer
6.00 pm	Two hours of unspecified tasks*
8.00 pm	Compline and retire

*Ramon noted:

> Evening hours may be used for walking, listening to music or anything missed during the day. The morning and afternoon periods are often interchanged because of occasional visitors or special writing commitments. Working in the vegetable garden, outdoor painting, walking and such activities vary according to season. The wonderful thing is that I can drop my spade, close my book or lay aside my manuscript or correspondence if I feel the Lord calling me into prayerful communion at any time. I am only here for love of him.[58]

The ascent from the main road up the rough narrow lane led to another world. Ramon always encouraged retreatants to walk this last half mile as if on pilgrimage, leaving behind the busyness of the city for the peace and rest of this holy place.

At the hermitage, Ramon was careful that the number of visitors was limited to those who sought counsel and advice. Social calls were discouraged as he was naturally reluctant to disturb the rhythm of prayer and work which were his daily routine. It was, however, to this quiet place on the top of the hill that a variety of people were drawn to seek advice, counsel and spiritual direction. Regular visitors included bishops, bankers and businessmen, priests and ministers, carers and seekers, and a steady stream of folk from a variety of religions and none, who were searching for some meaning to the life they were called to live. Ramon gently directed them, encouraged them and prayed for them. Chris Powell writes:

> I remember the way in which he would never criticise me, but was never afraid to speak truth and challenge in a disarmingly frank and amused way, which invited me into addressing whatever he had observed. While living and working in Coventry in my 20s and 30s, I would regularly take myself to Glasshampton for a few days, usually needing to make progress on a writing project or some other piece of work that was proving recalcitrant. While there, he would welcome me to make whatever use of the friary I needed, while joining in with the brothers' work and offices. He would also always use these opportunities to encourage my meagre attempts to engage in contemplation and meditation. Whenever I protested that I was doing what I could, he would nod vigorously and exclaim, 'Ah yes, the hidden life of prayer!' then, after a born actor's pause, he would add 'Very hidden!'

> Ramon often wrote me long and moving letters. Having known my father and mother at the time of my birth, he was about as close to being my godfather that good nonconformists could get. Of all that he wrote to me, however, what I remember is that he remembered to write. Even when I didn't immediately reply. What is more, he remembered not just me and what was happening in my life but also the lives around me. I was never in any doubt that, even when at the most isolated parts of his life, he remembered me and prayed for me, as he did for many others. This, of course, is the fundamental thing that makes us human, that we are known and remembered and so can relate. Ramon had a gift for making those he knew feel more fully human, and in that, more fully part of the divine. He never shied away from the differences between us but those

were miniscule in contrast to the way he came alongside me and helped me feel we were fellow travellers, whatever our separate roads.

Ramon kept up his letter-writing, and the correspondence he received in return was prolific. In these letters, he would share his everyday experiences, comment on the progress of his vegetable patch, recommend his latest book or simply provide valuable words of encouragement. Frequently, he would offer examples of God's guidance in his own life. It wasn't until 1999 that he exchanged his ancient typewriter for a Starwriter Word Processor, after much persuasion from his friends! Sadly, but understandably, because of the privacy of their contents, all his correspondence was destroyed after his death. His writings leave us in no doubt that, when he writes about prayer, he is writing from his own experience. He is practical. He often emphasises the importance of preparation for prayer and the need to relax and rest the body in order that the mind is adjusted to receive whatever the gift of God might be in contemplation or meditation. In *A Hidden Fire,* he writes:

> The Christian ideal is that the purified and enlightened spirit vitalises and guides the body, so that the whole person is dedicated to God in love and joy. 'So that we do not lose heart, though our outward nature is wasting away, our inner nature is being renewed day by day' (2 Corinthians 4:16).

> The biblical doctrine of salvation was never meant to indicate merely the rescue of the soul from the consequences of sin. The scope is much wider than that and has to do with 'spirit, soul and body' and Jesus is the Saviour of the body.[59]

He was disciplined in keeping fit; walking, jogging and cycling were important for him and he loved swimming and looked forward to a 'dip' in one of the Gower beaches when on his annual leave. For him, body and mind were intrinsically connected and had to be kept in tune. He urged people who are serious about their prayer life to spend time in preparation. If the body is to be offered as part of our worship, he argues, it has a particular part to play in prayer and in helping us to be attentive and aware of God's presence. Stillness and silence were seen as essential requisites:

> If one cannot wait upon God in silence and be still before him, then it is simply true that no life of prayer will follow.[60]

He recalls the stillness of Jesus, the quality of peace and rest which he communicated, and reminds his readers that not only did Jesus call his disciples apart to a desert place, but he himself frequently sought solitude on the lake, on the mountain top, in the Garden of Gethsemane and often continued all night in prayer. Jesus was his example as he himself entered into silence and solitude. In the opening chapter of *Deeper into God,* he urges his readers to make space for God:

> If you take this book seriously and begin to order your life in spending time and making space for God, then the pattern of prayer will lead you into a more contemplative orientation. The positive spiritual, psychical and physical results will make you a better human being, combining the blessings which St Paul envisages in his advice to Timothy, his son in the faith: 'Train yourself in godliness; for while bodily training is of some value, godliness is of value in every way, as it holds promise for the present life and also for the life to come.'[61]

Ramon's teaching about prayer included hints on posture. While recommending the use of a prayer stool (of which he made many), he recognised that no particular posture is suitable for all. He makes suggestions about breathing in prayer – all part of a readiness to meet the living God. In all his teaching on spirituality, he recognised the difficulties of people living busy lives finding time to be apart with God and encouraged them to go on a retreat for the first time. Always acknowledging the privilege of living the hermit life, he recognised the natural fear of solitude and silence, while gently inviting people into the presence of God where they would find healing, growth and renewal. *Deeper into God* is a practical guide to going on retreat with helpful advice, particularly for those making a retreat for the first time. He was always anxious to emphasise the importance of *experiencing* God:

> Life in God is meant to be an *experienced* life, leading to an awareness of the divine presence as well as the divine absence. Retreat opens out into that experiential dimension in which one learns not only with the mind, but also in the heart, the powerful meaning of the gospel of death and resurrection.[62]

So the life at the little hermitage, with its daily rhythm of prayer and work, continued; the vegetables flourished, the seasons came and went, a trickle of visitors rang the small bell at the gate of the enclosure and returned to their homes and places of work inspired and refreshed.

The great 'Hullo'!

On 29 August 1998, those on his mailing list received a letter from Ramon with the news that he was unwell. After a shortened visit to Swansea, he had returned to Glasshampton. His annual two weeks' leave was cut short for, almost as soon as he arrived, he was taken ill. On the Sunday evening at Rhosili church at the tip of the Gower Peninsula, which he knew so well, he addressed a group of pilgrims from the parish of Cockett in Swansea. The parishioners remember it as an inspiring service at which he spoke about a life of walking with our Lord and the joy of recording in his prayer journal God's faithfulness and his happiness. The following night, spent with his friend Ieuan at Mumbles, 'retention' began with the result that he was admitted to Morriston Hospital, where at one time he had been a nurse. There he underwent a series of tests and prostate cancer was diagnosed. He was to have had further treatment, but he desperately wanted to return to Glasshampton. After explaining his situation to the medical staff, he was discharged on the Friday evening with the recommendation that he should contact his GP immediately on his return with a view to getting an appointment with a urologist as soon as possible. On the following Monday, he met with his GP and it was obvious that his condition was more serious than was first thought and that his treatment would either be radical surgery or manipulative hormone therapy. In his letter, he told us that he was in good heart and felt 'enfolded within the love of the Lord'. He had a visit from Mike Mitton (of the Acorn Healing Trust), who celebrated the Eucharist and anointed him during the community mass which Ramon described as 'a good and healing experience and I look to the Lord for his healing grace'.

There followed a long period of radiotherapy and treatment, with dark periods of pain and discomfort. In an article he later wrote for *Guidelines,* which wasn't published until 2002, he described the effectiveness of the constant practice of the Jesus Prayer:

> Indeed, in writing such words about the diagnosis, it is only honest to say that the depths of mystical awareness and the love of God has been increasingly profound. I am writing this not to say that the use of the Jesus Prayer in sickness is less effective than I had thought, but to affirm that I now find that its direction need not be towards physical healing (though this may well be included), but in a more spiritual dimension in our own and other's lives.[63]

Ramon describes the Jesus Prayer:

> The Jesus Prayer is simply part of the church's rich life of prayer and adoration. It expresses humankind's yearning and response to the Spirit of God. It is part of the deep river of prayer that flows from the fecundity of grace, through the cosmic order, and returns to the heart of God, our ultimate home and rest.[64]

The prayer originates in the cry of the blind man begging on the Jericho Road:

> They told him: 'Jesus of Nazareth is passing by.' Then he shouted, 'Jesus, Son of David, have mercy on me.'
> LUKE 18:37–38 (NIV)

'Jesus, Son of the Living God, have mercy on me, a sinner' are words which Christians have made their prayer, repeating the sentence over and over again, for many centuries and is part of the tradition of the Orthodox Church which is now widely used by Christians in the Western church.

In spring 2000, Ramon was writing of the awareness of the love and healing that surrounded him:

The medical care and expertise and the basic life within the community of SSF is a constant reality, together with the prayers and love of all those who are my friends and loved ones.

He apologised for his inability to reply to the 200 pieces of mail he had received. It is obvious that he lacked the energy and concentration to do this, but there was encouraging news from his GP and the nursing team, who felt positive about the results of the treatment that he had been receiving.

In one of his letters, he comments:

One of the things that has happened to me at a new level since that stark diagnosis last August is the fact that I need not worry about how or where I should be or minister. I should simply be here for the Lord and for myself, and he will do the rest. We can do more for our poor sin-stricken and suffering world in this way than running around as we used to trying to plug the holes in the dyke. The Lord has those who need to do that in that stage in their lives. But now, from a deeper depth of prayer and love, let it overflow and affect the world.[65]

Reluctantly but realistically, Ramon soon moved from his hut and its enclosure to a room in the tower of the monastery where he was able to retain that silence and solitude which had become so important to him. There were some secret tears and a sense of bereavement at parting from his hut, but there was also the recognition that this was inevitable as he became weaker. He also decided now to withdraw his commitment to write a book on the life of St Francis. He did, however, choose to go ahead with his plans to co-author a book on the Jesus Prayer with Bishop Barrington-Ward. This was to be his final task in which his last days are movingly recorded for us.

Simon Barrington-Ward was formerly General Secretary of what was then known as the Church Missionary Society and subsequently

Bishop of Coventry (1985–1997). It was through a small book on the Jesus Prayer[66] that he came into contact with Ramon, who had earlier written a similar book. They decided to share together their experiences of the Jesus Prayer, subsequently published with the title *Praying the Jesus Prayer Together* (BRF, 2001). The book is the fruit of 20 years of using the prayer by both authors. It all came together when the bishop and Ramon set a week apart to further explore the Jesus Prayer at Glasshampton. The week was in September 1999, by which time Ramon's condition was rapidly deteriorating. It must have meant great effort on his part to cope with pain and discomfort and yet he was able to make his contribution to the work. Bishop Simon stayed at the nearby monastery, where he joined the brothers every day for their Morning Office before crossing over to the hermitage and entering Ramon's chapel hut to spend time praying the prayer together. Afterwards, they would move to the living hut next door where, after a cup of coffee, they would share in a time of reflection. Bishop Simon writes:

> On the first morning, I spoke the prayer aloud. The second morning, he did. We would always begin the prayer with an invocation to the Holy Spirit. Ramon mentioned that the tuft of wool on the end of the Orthodox 'prayer rope' could be seen as a symbol of Pentecost, of the Spirit opened up to us by the cross itself and drawing us through the cross into the life of the Trinity. So we would take our prayer ropes and hold the tuft between thumb and forefinger as we began with an invocation of the Holy Spirit. Thus, as the prayer was spoken, with each saying of it, we took hold of each knot in turn round the rope until we came back to the start.[67]

As the week progressed, Ramon was in continuous pain and fatigue, but he persevered and both writers attest to the fact that that was a week to remember as an encounter with the living Christ.

Praying the Jesus Prayer Together leaves us in no doubt that both authors throughout the years found this way of praying a wonderful expression of adoration and intercession. Bishop Simon writes of the ways in which he introduced the prayer to the parishes in his diocese where much was happening. He and his staff, however, came to see that there was a missing dimension. There was an urgent need to undergird all these exciting activities by prayer and a deepening of the spiritual life of themselves and the people of the diocese:

> We need our church to become the kind of place to which we could gladly take a friend who is a complete outsider to the church, because the kind of welcome they would receive and the kind of worship they would experience would have a depth and genuineness and openness that would truly constitute a kind of homecoming. Here would be the same kind of anticipation of the goal towards which humanity is struggling. A church rooted and grounded in prayer and in the hidden contemplation of the presence of Christ would have a powerful attraction to it. The sense of the love of God poured out would be palpable, not because the members were trying self-consciously to make it so, but because they were naturally, gently and easily held in that love by the stream of prayer that flowed through their shared life.[68]

The bishop was convinced that this could happen and, as a consequence, used every opportunity to introduce individuals and groups to the Jesus Prayer. Meanwhile, Ramon had also been teaching novices and retreatants the value of the prayer. He writes about conducting a retreat:

> When I lead a retreat, on the last evening I invite everybody to come together in the chapel. We then embark on a corporate participation in the Jesus Prayer. I have usually led this, and the others, as in the monastery, join in silently, not speaking but yet following the prayer 'with the mind in the heart'. We are focusing on the presence and person of Jesus, crucified and risen, and with us always 'even to the end of time' (Matthew 28:20). We seek together to leave all other mental activity

behind and simply to be still in the presence. As we have already experienced, this inevitably becomes, so to speak, a symphony with two movements – of rejoicing in the presence of Jesus Christ, and, as we address him as Son of God, being led into the presence of God as the loving parent ('Abba') to whom the Son brings us as the Holy Spirit prays within us.[69]

The 'week of glory', as Ramon and Simon called it, soon came to an end. The book had now been planned and it was time for each of the authors to go their separate ways to put on paper the thoughts and reflections they had shared together and which they wanted to share with others. In May of the following year, Simon received a telephone call from Brother Raymond Christian, who had taken on the role of Ramon's carer, telling him that he was now much weaker with a changed blood count and difficulties in having transfusions. Simon went straight over to Glasshampton to visit him to find that, although the colour had drained from his face, he was still the same old Ramon, welcoming his friend with a firm handshake and a warm smile, and enthusiastically recalling events that had taken place in hospital where he had spent a few days. He also shared a recent dream:

> The Lord had approached him over a narrow delicate bridge and, standing on it, had beckoned him to come across. 'I have come to fetch you,' he said. Ramon was full of peace and excitement at this word. But he asked the Lord if he could stay a little and see Simon, then, the next day his sister, who was coming to be with him, and later Donald, his spiritual director who was also coming to say goodbye.[70]

As the visit drew to a close, Ramon pointed to a wire basket at the foot of the bed which contained his typescript for the half of the book he had written. 'I hope you won't mind,' he said, 'but I've finished it and it's complete, just waiting for your half! You see, I was in a bit of a hurry!' Then he gave his friend a copy of his *Fullness of Joy,* asking him to read the last three chapters: 'Joy in life and death',

'Joy in crossing over' and 'Judgement and eternal joy', which now had a special significance for him. They prayed the Jesus Prayer and blessed each other. Ramon, in spite of his weakness, was still smiling and chuckling which prompted his visitor to exclaim,

> 'I don't know why, but it seems so strange, somehow unbelievable, that I am saying "Goodbye" to you in this life and won't see you here any more after this!' He clasped my hand saying, 'Well, of course it is strange! Still, there it is, Simon. This is the last journey, you know.' But then almost immediately a twinkle came into his eye and his face lit up, as it often would when he was about to express some vital new thought. 'But when we get to the end of this – there'll be...' and he raised his voice suddenly, and almost shouted, 'a big HULLO!' And he laughed and gripped my hand. Still laughing, we parted really merrily after all. It was impossible to be sad. I have never before nor since come away from a deathbed actually feeling exhilarated as I did then, despite the sharp sense of loss. I knew that most of all I would miss that affectionate laughter, that assurance of an ultimate 'divine comedy' in which we were all implicated.

On the night of 5 June 2000, Ramon peacefully slipped away. His requiem Eucharist celebrated ten days later was, as he would wish, full of joy. His coffin was brought into the quire by his Franciscan brothers. There, surrounded by his sister and her family and a multitude of friends from all over the UK, the service began. As I had heard him sing 'Love Divine' in Canterbury Cathedral years ago, now I could almost hear him lustily singing the first hymn 'Bread of Heaven' (Cwm Rhondda). The service was introduced by his friend, Ieuan Lloyd, who was able to bring to the vast congregation personal memories of one who to the end had served his Lord with love and joy, and had brought to so many people a hope that would change their lives. The requiem included a reading from Ramon's book, *A Month with St Francis.* His spiritual director, Canon Donald Allchin, gave the eulogy. After Communion, members of the Franciscan community encircled the coffin as it was censed and sprinkled with holy water. A brother read verses from Charles Wesley's hymn, which Ramon had requested to be sung at his funeral to the Welsh tune, Trewern, which the organ played in the background. (I suspect that it wasn't sung because the compilers of the service were doubtful of the familiarity of the tune to the congregation!):

Rejoice for a brother deceased,
Our loss is his infinite gain;
A soul out of prison released,
And freed from its bodily chain:
With songs let us follow his flight,
And mount with his spirit above,
Escaped to the mansions of light,
And lodged in the Eden of love.

Our brother the haven hath gained,
Out-flying the tempest and wind,
His rest he hath sooner obtained,
And left his companions behind,
Still tossed on a sea of distress,
Hard toiling to make the blessed shore,
Where all is assurance and peace,
And sorrow and sin are no more.

There all the ship's company meet
Who sailed with the Saviour beneath,
With shouting each other they greet,
And triumph over trouble and death:
The voyage of life at an end,
The mortal infliction is past;
The age that in heaven they spend
For ever and ever shall last.[71]

The service ended on a triumphant note as we all joined in singing the Easter hymn 'Thine be the glory'. After his cremation, his remains were taken to be buried alongside his brothers at the cemetery in Hilfield.

In a Lent talk, which was broadcast on Radio Devon in March 1985, Ramon spoke about humility:

> I can't think of myself as particularly humble – I mean, who can? So I asked 'Why?' I was told; 'You are a Franciscan and you ought to be humble!' Well, what does one say to that? The Franciscan habit, grey or brown, is the colour of the earth, the soil, and the soil is *humus*, from which the word humility comes. In Latin, *humus* is the ground, and as he lay dying, St Francis asked that he be laid naked on the ground, that he might return as humble and naked as he had come into the world.

Ramon was, above all, a humble man – gifted in so many ways, not least in that deep spirituality which was rooted in scripture and centred on Christ. He was a man of prayer. Yet he had both his feet firmly on the ground, keeping abreast with national and international affairs by means of his radio so that his prayers for the needs of the world were informed and up to date, fully aware of the problems facing those on the perimeter of society and anxiously praying for the renewal of the church. For him, it was unthinkable to separate the spiritual life from the practical aspects of living and surviving; he was possessed by what is often described as a holistic spirituality which impinges on everything. Chris Powell writes:

> One clear memory I have of Ramon is of him arranging to meet me in Swansea city centre one Saturday lunchtime when I was a teenager. He knew I was finding some things difficult at school and elsewhere, and I was looking forward to talking with him. He bought us both chips and we went to sit and eat and talk in Castle Gardens. We had only just sat down when he spied a homeless man – what we then used to call *wayfarers* – crouched dejectedly in a corner. He leapt up, roused the chap and brought him to sit with us, passing over half our chips.

I don't remember anything of what Ramon and I spoke about that day, but I was forcibly struck by the demonstration that it wasn't possible for us to sit there talking about spiritual things, while another human sat nearby alone, destitute. It was the most normal, natural thing for Ramon to welcome this stranger into our lunch and conversation. This was incarnational spirituality at work. If I hadn't fully understood what that meant before then, I did after.

In extracts from his writings which follow, we are privileged to observe his inner journey with Christ in God, a journey of discovery, transformation and transfiguration in which he sets his eyes on Christ. Although the latter part of his life was mostly in seclusion, he was still part of the world with all its problems and conflicts. The word 'transformation' was often on the lips of Donald Allchin, and it must have been a quality which he and Ramon discussed very frequently. Transformation, transfiguration, is a process which inevitably takes place when we contemplate Jesus' life, ministry, death and resurrection, all of which, with the help of the Spirit, cause us to become more like him. Those hours spent in prayer in the tiny hut in the grounds of Hilfield, in the winter and spring on Anelog overlooking Bardsey, in the peaceful field adjoining Tymawr and finally in the enclosure at Glasshampton, were moments of drawing close to God and, in Christ, beholding his glory. A humble man and a holy man; but his holiness didn't separate him from people. In fact, it drew him *to* people, because he saw in all with whom he came into contact a spark of the divine. It was in his holiness that he found joy.

At his requiem, his friend Ieuan said of him:

He had faults, though I would have gladly exchanged mine for his. His judgement faltered when it came to a bargain. He would buy batteries that lasted only minutes because they were cheap. When he was Guardian at Glasshampton, he used to buy provisions from Bookers. He would be delighted to find that some things were five for the price of four! But it had nothing to do with him owning anything. The Bishop of Glasgow said to him with admiration when he was leaving, having been attached to the cathedral for four years, 'Ramon, you came with a rucksack and you are leaving with a rucksack.' Ramon resisted modern technology with one exception – a microwave given to him by his sister.

Ramon would have hated to be put on a pedestal for, as we have seen, his life demonstrated a humble spirit, one who was completely open to God and whose one aim in life through his prayer, his writings and his encounters with people, was to open others to God. I doubt whether he would ever have approved of a book being written about him, so I ask his forgiveness and hope that he will understand my longing to share with others what he so effectively shared with us. He always reflected that wholesome holiness was devoid of all false piety and rooted in the Christ-life. What Celano says of Francis, that great master of holiness, however much he would contradict it, can be said of Ramon:

> He was a most eloquent man, a man of cheerful countenance, of kindly aspect; he was immune of cowardice, free of insolence. His speech was peaceable, fiery and sharp; his voice was strong, sweet, clear and sonorous. His skin was delicate, his flesh very spare... Because he was very humble, he showed all mildness to all, adapting himself usefully to the behaviour of all. The most holy amongst the holy, among sinners he was one of them.[72]

LETTERS

I feel it a great privilege to wear the habit of St Francis and long to be devoted to our dear Lord as he was – to rejoice and grieve at his passion and death upon the cross, and to exult in his glorious resurrection – to adore him in prayer and sacrament, and tell the good news all around the world that the love of Jesus includes everybody, and the Father's heart is open to all. You know that my evangelical background has combined with catholicity in my experience and I find a very wonderful combination of the two streams running together in prayer. I find myself sometimes in St Claire's Chapel here... and in the quietness and darkness I find myself singing before the Lord many of the old evangelical hymns which have meant so much in my Christian experience in days gone by and have returned with fresh vigour to communicate again the love of Jesus in word and sacrament. This one, for instance:

My Jesus I love Thee, I know Thou art mine;
For Thee all the pleasure of sin I resign;
My gracious Redeemer, my Saviour art Thou,
If ever I loved Thee, my Jesus, 'tis now.

I love Thee because Thou hast first loved me,
And purchased my pardon when nailed to the tree;
I love Thee for wearing the thorns on Thy brow,
If ever I loved Thee, my Jesus, 'tis now.

I know the hymn is not good poetry – even doggerel – but it expressed to me, as a young Christian, something of the love that wells up in my heart for our Lord Jesus – and still does so!

Hilfield Friary, 28 January 1979

I know that it was only 20 December when I was clothed as a Franciscan novice, but it does seem a long time ago, and certainly I feel it an immense privilege to be in the habit and in the Society, though there continues to be that restlessness about my perspective and understanding of life, that will, I'm sure, continue with me throughout my life. I have recently begun to think about it much more in terms of the old Welsh (indeed the whole Celtic) monastic pattern. St David would go off in his coracle to some lonely place or island and be alone with God in prayer, and then when the Spirit moved him he would go off and preach and teach with great fervour. It was a 'peripatetic' (walking about) life and ministry. I only hope that SSF will be able to put up with this kind of individualism.

Life here is very busy, but I do seem to have been making more interior progress – perhaps it is tied up with the fact that over the last two years I have been 'marking time', not quite sure where I belonged or where my roots were to go down, and now it does seem that I am in the right place to grow. Various deep and hidden voices speak concerning the life of prayer constantly, but SSF is becoming more aware of the dimension of prayer needing to be strengthened within the society, – and of that I am glad.

Hilfield Friary, undated

When it comes to saying something about the spiritual and psychical side of the life, it is difficult to know what to say and how to say it. If you know me, you realise that I am not often at a loss for words, but this experience was one which I have long looked forward to, and which encapsulated my deepest longings and desires for God in love and prayer, and I hardly know what to say about it. There were times of intense longing and joy, times of darkness, conflict and ambiguity, and shades of *accidie* between. But it was all necessary, an experiment which has pointed me in a certain direction more clearly, confirming my feelings about contemplative prayer and my involvement in such a life and vocation, although the details have not been spelled out.

There were times when I was carried through Gospel scenes, participating in the life of Jesus; times of study which brought me into a deeper awareness of the presence of God, answering Hoskyns' question affirmatively: 'Can we bury ourselves in a lexicon and arise in the presence of God?' And there were times when I was drawn into the beginnings of a more contemplative way which my heart longs for, and for which this period of solitude prepared me.

Hilfield Friary (after his first six months in solitude
in a hut in the grounds), October 1982

What situations I get myself into. Here I am perched on the side of Anelog mountain, in a tiny 100-year-old stone cottage with no one in sight, sea below and sky above, and a beautiful white woolly sheep looking at me through the window – how they survive I cannot imagine, and how sure-footed they are on the cliff paths – one slip and down they would tumble into the sea far below...

This is the most wonderful time, and yet the most crazy. I am at the tip of the Lleyn Peninsula – and at 4.30 am this morning I was wrapped in a blanket saying my night office, wishing I had filled a hot water bottle! It is so cold today that I lit my little foot square egg-fuel fire. There are no trees, so I got some of the gnarled heather roots lying around, and surprisingly they are good kindling so I have a tiny fire today – I think I shall only have it for Sundays and very high days as I can't afford it – but more than that I don't want to be soft (little hope here!).

This is the second six months of my solitude experiment, and when Mother Mary Clare said I should do it away from the friary, and in the winter and in an exposed and cold place, she knew what she was talking about – do you think she's trying to dissuade me? But I went out at 7.00 am to see the dawn streaking the eastern sky over the Peninsula – Bardsey is opposite – the island of 20,000 saints and this whole Peninsula is soaked in the hermit life and prayer – the Celtic tradition still lives. Last evening, I sat high above the sea and played on my recorder 'My Song is Love Unknown', and the earth and the sea and sky received the music into itself as part of the whole patchwork of love and prayer and solitude…

It is strange in some ways to know that my time of 'soap box' communicating is drawing to a close. As it is now, I feel that I shall not do another mission – I suppose that is not so because SSF will see to that in the immediate future, but I must say that it is becoming more and more difficult to keep up such external and verbose ministry. It seems to me that whereas I swam out from the SSF harbour and was carried out with the current of apostolic work and evangelism with a quiet undercurrent of prayer, now the undercurrent has become the main pull and I am more and more unable to do the preaching/ missions, etc. part.

Mount Pleasant, Anelog, Aberdaron, 16 November 1983

Yes, you also see the importance of my parents' death. We were so close to each other, and I miss them in a profound way, but I see now that it was right for them both to go together, though I had hoped especially for my mother to have a few years of relative peace and joy. I had a special sense of their presence with me about a fortnight ago, as I stood at the altar to receive Communion. There was a distinct sense of my father on my left and my mother on my right. The communion of saints is more precious to me now. You see that now I am free to explore the possibility of a vocation which has drawn and lured me for a number of years. I knew you would read the paper I sent you with discernment and understanding. I have had positive feedback from it, and the sad and yet providential thing is that Mother Mary Clare wrote me an important letter on 27 July, and I called to see her last Thursday in Oxford, and that morning she had lapsed into unconsciousness and was dying. I knelt and prayed for her then, and she died on Sunday morning. I shall go to the funeral tomorrow and see Canon Donald Allchin there. All this dovetails in a remarkable way…

Glasshampton, 17 August 1988

My book on Thomas Merton will be out in February. It is to be called *Soul Friends: A journey with Thomas Merton,* and will be a patchwork quilt of spirituality, theology, soul-direction and personal witness. Then I am going to write a NOVEL – a genre I have wanted to explore, and I think I have found the right man – yes, you've guessed, Jacopone da Todi, for in his life is adventure, quest, violence, sensuality, politics, religion, excommunication, imprisonment, all in the context of the love and mercy of God. I have much to say about him which is not explicitly historical, but which I have come to believe about his life – and the message is exciting and important!

Glasshampton, 30 December 1988

I've just finished the manuscript for the second book, which will probably be called *Deeper into God,* and is a theological and practical handbook on retreats. I extracted a chapter this week to send to those who are in some kind of 'direction' relationship with me... I wonder what Marshall-Pickering will say about this one, as it carries the Catholic dimension much further than the last, though, of course, it is more solidly evangelical in its biblical sections.

I have had many scores of appreciative letters – hardly a week goes by even now when someone does not write positively, sometimes two or three letters a week. They have all been positive – save one, and that one (a Calvinist Baptist) was so full of bigotry and hatred that I couldn't believe my eyes – well, yes, I could, but my first reaction was to reply in two or three brief paragraphs courteously, but then I took the letter and realised that it wasn't a true reflection of how I felt – my real reaction was, 'Don't be so daft...' So I didn't send the letter and put his letter into the basket. If I'd said, 'Don't be so daft', he wouldn't have appreciated it, I think. But it does make me sad. I do feel a bit of a heel, I think, because no reply – the effect of silence could be coals of fire on his head...

I think I realise a little more that the best commendation and defence of truth is love. I mean that I want to continue to live and speak positively about truth wherever it may be found, and commend it with enthusiasm and joy. If others do not find it so, then so be it – I am not infallible, and temperaments and intellectual viewpoints are different, and the Lord has ways past my finding out. But I feel I can continue to commend life-giving bread and wine as I find it...

No details of place or date

In August, I shall be going off to test my vocation to the eremitical [hermit] life, and this is something which has ever more been pressing upon me over the last decade. Even from a child, I have been drawn to solitude. I suppose it was the Evangelical and Baptist tradition which brought out the powers of communication in me. I am grateful for that because I do love people and as you know there is a really gregarious side to my personality.

Always, too, I have been in a position of leadership and counsel, and I realise that, humanly speaking, if I stayed within the communicative world it would lead to a place of leadership which would be foreign to what the Lord is calling me to. I remember when I left Scotland to join SSF, one young couple said, 'Why are you going? If you stayed in Scotland, in ten years you would be shortlisted for a bishop.' I think now that would be the hand of death upon me. God knows there is a need for godly and consecrated men in the episcopate, but I'm not one of them. Then in our Society I was elected to the General Chapter and was the first in the history of the Society to refuse! Indeed (and this letter is not for public consumption), I have felt a powerful voice within me saying: 'Be silent. Or I shall silence you!' That is not a threat, but the loving counsel of One who calls me, ever calls me. I am endeavouring to obey, though it's taken a long time. But now I have given up being Guardian. I did my last mission for the Clyne Deanery (ten churches) last month, and my last School of Prayer last week. So I have almost an empty diary so that I can give my full attention to Glasshampton over the last month or two – especially with the novices and helping in the new Guardian, Amos.

The 'I shall silence you' idea could well have been a physical or mental restraint if I had not obeyed – it's as clear as that to me, so although I've had scores of letters/verbal message that I should not give up preaching/teaching/retreats, etc., it is a matter of obedience for me now...

Glasshampton, 8 June 1990

I've been here since the end of August, and we are now on the verge of 1991, so let me say a few things about my present situation... The convent at Tymawr is an Anglican contemplative Order called the Society of the Sacred Cross and is Benedictine in its spirituality, now having two brothers integrating into its former 'sisters only' community (pray for them, Brian and Jack). I am on their land, though it is fields away from the convent, through gates and over hedges in a plum orchard which looks down on a huge field sloping down to a small stream, then a narrow road and a forest of trees up into the hills which separates this area from Trelech. I live a solitary life, though I do work for the community in the early morning or during the day when there is no one around – daily watering, feeding and cleaning the hens, some gardening, wood-chopping, painting and decorating, and I have a 'buffer brother' (Jack) and we have a box where we leave notes for one another and on a Friday he leaves me some eggs/cheese/vegetables. My timetable varies according to light, but at present is something like this:

4.30 am Meditation and prayer

6.30 am Up to convent to do hens, packing refuse for collection and work indicated in various notes (e.g. burning rubbish/clearing a barn, etc.)

7.30 am Back to caravan, ablutions, SSF Morning Prayer, breakfast

9.30 am Morning for reading/study/writing (e.g. I'm learning Welsh at last!) and some Greek text, etc. Keeping up theological reading

12.30 pm Midday SSF prayer

1.00 pm Preparation and eating of main meal

2.30 pm Afternoon work: bookbinding, prayer-stool making, icon mounting, domestic chores, painting and decorating for convent (e.g. I'm painting the print-room starting tomorrow; some days jogging/walking/cycling – roads are deserted)

5.30 pm Cup of coffee

6.00 pm SSF Evening Prayer and meditation followed by light reading/music

8.00 pm Compline and bed

I've known great turbulence and great stillness since being here. I've been drawn to call into question so many things which have seemed to be the primary things in my life and ministry. It's a matter of the first being last and the last first, I suppose, and I'm finding that I'm missing people very much – more than during my first and second six-month periods. This does not argue for packing up, but rather measures the sacrifice which is costly to me – and this is increasingly so. How trite it would seem for me to answer the question: 'Are you lonely?' by replying that I was alone but not lonely. It would not be true, for human loneliness has always been part of my life, and very much so at present. But in a strange way, that casts me back on to the Lord who seems to have called me to this place at this time for his own purposes – and his purposes are always purposes of love.

Tymawr Convent, 31 December 1990

The strange thing is that I have now been able to 'let go' my various ministries – and they were piling up, as you know – and though there has been great joy in communication at all its levels according to my gregarious nature, and though I miss people greatly and miss many of the simple joys of sharing with congregations, groups and individuals, yet it has been right for me to come here, and to remain here into the second year. I don't know whether it is a matter of being like Elijah for three years at the brook Cherith or if it will go on into the unknown future. Whatever is true, then let it be. There are some moments when the 'old Adam' feels the sadness of turning down some invitations (which still arrive!) One came some months back from SSJE [The Society of St John the Evangelist] in Connecticut, Mass. USA, asking me to conduct their week's community retreat there next June, and of course there would grow up around that much lecturing, preaching, etc. I immediately knew that it had to be 'no' but I could imagine such a trip, though I'm sure that if I did go, that would lead to another roundabout of the kind of ministries which are not right for me now…

Tymawr Convent, 18 December 1991

I thought of you today as I walked the Stations of the Cross here in my enclosure, and enclose the booklet *Remember Me* that I used – hoping it will reach you by Good Friday so that you may use it then.

And I also commend to you the prayer of Ramon Lull that he prayed before the crucified Jesus:

When I am wholly confounded, and know not where to look or where to turn, then do your eyes behold me, and in those eyes which wept for our sin, and that heart which was wounded and cleft for us, do I seek and implore my salvation. And in those tears, and in that love and mercy – there do I find my health and my salvation, and there only.

Tymawr Convent, 10 April 1992

Thank you for your prayers over my decision either to remain here for an extended period or to take up the invitation to Bardsey Island. That invitation, as you can imagine, was full of challenge and adventure – and the island which would be cut off for the whole of the winter, with just two other people there would have been a hermit's delight (with darker repercussions, too, I'm sure). The strange thing is that I have not felt that interior affirmation that I look for in making such a decision. It seems to me that I have laid a good foundation here since 1990 and my roots have gone down so that the fruit is beginning to appear, and STABILITY seems the right word from my point of view and as a witness to and from SSF. I don't want them to feel that I want to go hiving off after every new invitation that comes along. I have refused two invitations for lectures/preaching, etc. in the USA for next year, and it looks as if I may be refusing the Bardsey invitation – though that is an infinitely more important decision. I have come to the conclusion that unless the Lord gives me a CLEAR word by vision/prophecy/counsel or whatever within the next two weeks or so, I should remain here. If so, in the spring I shall be building a stone cell on to the derelict barn in the next field. It means laying a concrete floor, knocking three windows into the existing three walls, and building a wall/door/window into the fourth side.

Tymawr Convent, 19 December 1992

I am moving back to my former balance, though B/P [blood pressure] is still up a bit. But I remember in 1966 having a medical before going to Zurich, and the GP saying then, 'Your B/P is a bit high.' I've known for some ten years or so that I have some hypertension, evident when chopping wood or hard digging by the 'hot and cold' symptoms, but I've said, 'Oh, everyone over 50 has some hypertension' and did nothing about it...

I have been thinking much over whether I should move back to the grounds of one of our own friaries or do the conversion of the barn here. It feels okay to get on with the latter in a month or two and I shall have the solid help of one of our Glasshampton friends who is a handyman. One of the lovely jobs I've been doing over the last two weeks is planting sapling trees/shrubs. The convent had a grant from the Forestry Commission to plant 1,000 in a large field surrounding the pond, and agri students from Usk college came to do 700 and left the rest to the gardener – so I have done about 130 – Dogwood,

Guelder, Blackthorn, Spindle, Hawthorn, Wayfaring, Ash, Lime, Cherry and Oak. How much I enjoy doing this, especially on my own – I feel I am planting for the future, with the prayer that the Lord will plant new seeds of hope and love in my heart! Yours too!

Tymawr Convent, 2 April 1993

I am moving next week back to Glasshampton after three years, and going to live in the grounds of Glasshampton in two huts (this time heated!). Anglia TV are doing a filming of Glasshampton, and Amos let slip that I would be there, so they asked for a five-minute interview. I said a gentle but firm 'No' with no possibility of a change of mind!…

You know I intended to convert a barn here into a stone cell, but as I went up some afternoons to pray in it, I could hear the text: 'Unless the Lord builds the house those who build it labour in vain' (Psalm 127:1). This perplexed me, and after a period of prayer and thought it became suddenly clear one afternoon that I should return to Glasshampton. I find a certain sadness in leaving this place, but I'm sure it is the right step, and all those with whom I share (especially 'my three wise men') believe it is the right step. So I shall celebrate the Eucharist for the sisters on Sunday, which will be exactly three years since I began here (29 August), so I shall preach on Elijah's three years at Cherith when the ravens sustained him. One commentator thinks that the 'ravens' were a community of spiritual nomads, so I shall share with the sisters Elijah's thoughts on leaving Cherith and the ravens!

I shall return to Glasshampton via Swansea to see my sister and relatives. And over the Sunday I shall preach at St James' Swansea as I've done for the last three years in my annual visit to Wendy, and this year I shall also take the assembly at Gors School. Mother Gillian had to be away for the Oblates' Conference here this year, so although I don't do anything liturgical I led the Conference (the ministry part) and left the liturgical part to the sisters and the chaplain. I told the story of two groups of amazing people:

- 3 centuries BC: The Taoist Fathers
- 3 centuries AD: The Desert Fathers

It went so very well, and I was happy to be ministering, though it is clear that this is no longer the primary part of my life...

I've just made a decision closing my eyes. All my correspondence of the last three years seems immense – and I've ditched it all – all the carbon copies of my replies too. It was no use going through them – the letters are some of them very precious – the stories of so many on their own pilgrimage – Catholics and Pentecostals, Quakers and Baptists – and even Anglicans! So I took the whole lot and pitched them into a black bag, as I did when I left Glasshampton – then it was six years! I hate doing it, but cannot carry it all around. My external preaching ministry practically ceased, but the correspondence due to my writing has increased...

Tymawr, 25 August 1993

Our friendship continues with joy and openness, humour and love unabated! Thanks for your birthday greetings – but when is *your* birthday – it's not fair that you've unearthed mine and I don't have (lost?) yours! Yes, I also remember you and me and so many others as we were in Baptist College days. Well, do you know the two images of you which are closest to me? First, when we were in the bus coming (or going) from the Ministerial Recognition Committee – was it in Bridgend? – when we were undergoing some 'inquiry' as to our suitability for Baptist College (or preaching or something), and we quietly agreed that we should simply be 'ourselves' and not put on any airs and graces, because we really had a basic and 'common' background anyway! The second picture is when you preached that wonderful sermon in Baptist College. It was either on the text: 'I am crucified with Christ...' or 'I bear in my body the marks of the Lord Jesus...' Also I have another image when I came to you in Water Street when you had something like quinsy and you were not at all well!

Let me tell you how things are here. I gave away my caravan, then gave up taking the medication which was making me very tired – I felt better without it! I'm still without it, and the new GP says that we'll give it a trial without, and my throat is also improving! Anyway, I preached and celebrated Eucharist for the SSC sisters… It was good and sad, but both realising the blessing the Lord had afforded us in being together in prayer and solitude, without any misunderstanding or negativity during the three years. Then I came here, found a bargain hut which was delivered and erected on 30 September, then with help I lined/insulated/hard boarded/painted/carpeted, and on St Francis' Day (4 October) we processed down with incense in the pouring rain, did a Jericho march around the enclosure, exorcising evil, asking the Lord's blessing on land, huts and me! And they left me! I am so grateful to the Lord for the continuation of this vocation, which is increasingly precious and yet difficult too. I spent time with Wendy and family – how good that was, Wendy and I are very close and we miss our parents so much. You have, perhaps, read the chapter 'Loving' in *Forty Days and Forty Nights*. You knew them and brought them to Glasshampton – I'm so grateful for that. I preached at St James', Swansea on the 12th – it was wonderful communicating again – tremendous feeling to have the congregation eating out of one's hand – dangerous, too, but so good if you have the word to preach! Then Gors School assembly and classes on the Monday – it was good for me to feel that my communicative ability remains – and yet I know it is no longer the primary thing…

I'm glad you feel positive about Glasshampton – it seems that this is general, and it is strange, but even though I'm in the shadow of the monastery, I can hardly hear the bell, and I've seen and heard no one since the 4th (now the 15th). My view is towards the acres of fields below, sweeping down to the woodlands, then rising up from the trees on the other side of the valley I see the tower of Astley Church where Frances Ridley Havergal wrote a lot of her hymns, near to the Dick Brook which opens into the Severn where she wrote: 'Like a river glorious/ Is God's perfect peace'.

Glasshampton, 15 October 1993

The two huts are standing up well – and did so through the rain, frost and windy storms of winter and now the burning sun. Today I sit outside between the two huts with my typewriter on my knee. The differences since I wrote are that I have now taken over all the vegetable garden work and extended it (a bit too much in my spring zeal!) so that it has required three hours a day lately, but I have broad, French and runner beans/beetroot/carrots/swedes/kohlrabi/spinach/cabbages… The veggie garden lies over the hedge from my hut and separates me from the lawn and monastery, so I am left to myself down here. I face wild fields, down to the woodlands with the tower of Astley Church rising in the distance. A neighbour made me a covered wooden 'iconostasis' for my giant icon of Our Lady of Vladimir to stand under a tree in the corner of my enclosure – and this is very beautiful and gives a sense of prayer and wonder to the place. And also a three-foot Celtic cross in oak which stands outside my prayer hut.

I've seen about five people a month, including two Buddhists lately – one of them is a Buddhist monk who, it seems, desires to join SSF. He found some of my books in his library at the Buddhist monastery, and wrote saying the person of Jesus was more and more precious to him, and could he come and talk. I wrote and said that he must not forsake the Buddhist four noble truths and eightfold path, for they are an expression of universal truth, but that he should grow in the love and knowledge of Christ – for I assured him that there are many who do not belong to the church but they are certainly in the kingdom. (I think you may agree with this piece of 'heresy' which is nearer the heart of God than many of our so-called orthodoxies!)

Physically, the last 18 months has shown me my finitude and mortality more clearly, but I'm glad that after leaving off the B/P medication my B/P went down nearly to normal (some medicines are worse than the disease!), and since the throat problem persisted, I went two weeks ago and saw the ENT fellow, from whom I received welcome reassurance. He said that my deviated septum (broken nose – which I believe happened when I got my head stuck in wooden banisters as a child and had to be sawn out!), had at last caused the inflammation of the mucous membrane at the back of the throat. Also the swelling which I thought was glandular was actually a muscular swelling oesophagus/trachea which was causing the discomfort in swallowing, but he said this would slowly subside given time. A number of people were presenting the latter symptoms and he didn't know why. I was assured by his 'don't know' as the GP was guessing that the whole lot were caused by an allergy to agricultural chemical fertiliser. I believe they do a lot of harm but was not convinced it was the basis of my symptoms. So I am much assured and live with what are left of my symptoms – for the method of healing prayer that I use is certainly of real value – if you are interested I'll send you the chapter in which I describe the method for others which will appear in a future book (it involved the larger of the Christ-icons which I sent you).

That brings me to writing. You know that the first year at Tymawr, I saw no one and did no writing. My spiritual director, Father Donald Allchin, felt that a 'measured' number of people per month, plus my writing, was good for my particular way of living out this life. So since then I've been writing. *Franciscan Spirituality* (SPCK) was published in May, and is doing well, though the cover is not of my choosing, yet some people like it. *The Way of Love: Following Christ through Lent and Easter* (HarperCollins) is a daily Lent book which will be published in December. I feel very joyful about this book, which has already been adopted by three dioceses for recommendation, and I believe it will do well on your bookstall! Then I have in mind a book which contains chapters on counsel which I give to people on prayer, meditation and getting one's whole life together in terms of soma, psyche and pneuma – in simpler language than that, but dealing with such matters as 'when the steam dries up' and 'how to discern between simple depression and the dark night'. Then I have in mind another book on the pattern of a week's retreat, like *Heaven on Earth,* but it will be based on the seven letters of the risen Christ in the Apocalypse

(Revelation 1—3), with seven vegetarian recipes from Greece and Asia Minor! The one complaint I've constantly received about my writing is that the recipes in *Heaven on Earth* contain enough for four people – I omitted to say that the amounts are made to last me for three meals!

There are 100 cows/calves in the next field and I can hear them hungrily munching as I write. Last evening I caught sight of the pure white barn owl who flies over my huts at dusk looking for mice/voles. He is a graceful creature; with at least a three-foot wingspan (maybe much more) and front-set wide eyes in those beautiful white circles. I glimpsed him last evening in my pyjamas, and got hold of my binoculars and rushed (quietly) to my seat which looks out on the extended field below me. He was there flying up and down the length of the field, searching the ground, and suddenly swooping for prey. I got him in my sights and from the bottom of the field, came nearer and nearer until he swooped right past me – so very beautiful a creature – almost too perfect to be real – somewhat ghostly in pure white with that typical and unique facial expression.

I shall be going on my annual trip out of my enclosure (apart from GP visits) during the last fortnight of August, to Swansea to see my sister and relatives, and shall preach at the Eucharist at St James' Church, Swansea on the 21st. It will be so very different a fortnight, seeing so many people, doing a lot of cycling and some swimming around the Gower Peninsula. The 'romantic author' Iris Gower was a teenage girlfriend of mine, and we've been in touch for about ten years now – and suddenly last year she wrote and said that she could not hold out against the Lord any longer and she went along to St Mary's to the Eucharist and found herself weeping in sorrow and joy. She has been reading my books and I've read three of her 'romantic novels', passing them on to my sister. Anyway, we are having a house Eucharist in her home with her friends, so that will be a joyful occasion, as she is now trying to integrate theology/spirituality with her writing...

I've recently read Brian Keenan's *An Evil Cradling* – a harrowing and powerful read which I thoroughly recommend and which shows the integrity of Keenan and the shining example of John McCarthy – though it is not a religious book. I recommended it to an evangelical book-manager fellow who comes to see me and he wrote and said that it had given him such a jolt that he had 'lost his faith' for a time – and I answered and said what a good thing that was! We are still in touch, and he is all the time realising the need to allow doubt and conflict to have its creative way in his thinking, experiencing and being.

Glasshampton, 30 July 1994

It is always good to hear from you, and especially as we had journeyed together over the Lent period. There were over 4,000 people doing the same, and I have had some very warm and joyful feedback from different parts of the church. I think this is one of the most encouraging things about my writing – that it continues to express and manifest a sense of unity in the 'mystical body' of Christ when outward divisions are often our shame. One group meeting in Nottingham sent me a signed card – meeting in a Methodist home, there were Baptists, Anglicans and Catholics involved... The publishers say that people are still buying it, though it is out of its 'sell-by' date until next Lent, and they asked if I would do another Lent book for 1997 – on a different scheme. To round off this area, I hear that *The Heart of Prayer* is due out in a fortnight. This is a book for those who have been on the way of prayer for some time... This will appear in spring of next year, with the new Lent book the following year. I am immediately cautioned to say 'if the Lord will'; for we well know how precarious it is to assume that we can do this or that when we will. Our times are in the Lord's hands, and perhaps we are at last learning that lesson of simple trust. The lovely thing is that if you or I were to die tomorrow, in spite of our sins and stupidities, we would be able to say, 'Our Jesus has done all things well,' for we can rest upon the divine grace which sustains us from first to last.

Glasshampton, 8 April 1995

There is a great deal that I want to share with you, and often long to see you. But must now settle in sending you what I call the 'Mary Letter'. Mary is a woman in her 60s who, some 15 years ago, after being assistant head of a Comprehensive School, felt the Lord calling her to give it up and retire to a cottage in the hills above Ludlow with her two Labradors and live a life of prayer with the Lord. This she did, and she comes to me annually. She is a wonderful and humanly warm person, and perhaps her holiness is because of her experiences of abuse and rejection as a child and teenager. Last visit she wanted to explore these areas which have wounded her and have taken years to look at, let alone heal. During our conversation she seized upon my comment that the divine Love was the heart of all things, and asked me to unpack it in terms of our, and her, lives. I said that I would say some things to her, and then choose to write a letter indicating my meaning. This letter does not include the personal things which we covered, so can be shared, and there are many things which are relevant to your own pilgrimage so I've enclosed a copy. Comment if you'd like to.

Glasshampton, 29 October 1996

I have recently erected and lined, painted and carpeted another hut within my enclosure. The problem was that my living hut was fine, and my second hut was doubling as a prayer and working hut, with my bookbinding, carpentry and icon mounting equipment there, so that one corner was for prayer and sacrament, and when three (sometimes four) novices came for their monthly Eucharist we were somewhat squashed. So we decided to have another 10 x 8-foot hut for a prayer hut. It is now in situ, with a giant icon of Our Lady of Vladimir on the altar table with the open Bible, and two beautiful icons of St Francis on either side in the corners. This morning Peder Liland and his wife Gure (Peder and I were together for the three years at Rüschlikon) came down at 7.00 am and we celebrated the Eucharist with joy and singing and tears: talk about the Toronto Blessing – it was the 'Glasshampton Blessing'! I haven't seen Peder for 28 or 29 years. They are both Norwegian and have been staying here for the last few days. Yesterday, we walked through the fields and woods up to St Peter's Church where Francis Ridley Havergal's father was Rector and where she was born, and having died at Caswell Bay, was brought back here and buried. So we stood around her grave, and sang 'Take my life and let it be...' – there were one or two people nearby, so I don't know what they thought was happening, then we prayed and gave thanks for her life, work and witness, and that we may follow the Saviour in such a way, with love and joy and compassion...

A little earlier on I mentioned the veil of death and the reality of the communion of saints. As you'll appreciate, people write to me in terminal illness for themselves or on behalf of loved ones. Sometimes I feel that I can clearly pray for healing/deliverance, and sometimes towards a good and gentle death, even accompanying them to the edge of the 'Jordan river' and commending them to angelic ministry into the nearer presence of our Lord until the Parousia, as they (and we) continue our further pilgrimage into union with God...

Glasshampton, 5 July 1997

I voted GREEN in the election (and that saves me being too disappointed with Tony Blair), and the Green Candidate came to see me this week – a nice woman in her 30s, vaguely Church of Scotland but in her youth she got caught up with Hari Krishna people who had become disillusioned with all religion. But she told me that she had read 50 pages of *Heaven and Earth* in one sitting and was continuing with it. She had a remarkable ability to ask questions on the nature of nature-mysticism and asked whether I believed in a kind of hierarchy of beings, and she was delighted when I said that I thought that the mineral kingdom was the basis from which ascended the animal and human kingdoms, and I saw no reason to stop there but that I believed that there was a whole chain of being(s) through the angelic orders, and that there was also a kingdom of darkness – and she agreed with that. It is amazing that there are secular people who believe more in spiritual realities than the people who occupy our Anglican and Baptist pews!

I am sorry to hear that you are not having a good time in terms of health. It is not easy to realise that one cannot do the things one used to. I am grateful for the measure of health which enables me to go on here, to dig over the veggie garden in the mornings, etc. But I have to acknowledge that something happened to me on that night in the caravan in Tymawr back in 1992, and before that I was firing on six cylinders but since then have been firing on four! But let me tell you a salutary experience I had in my two weeks away in Swansea in August. I miss the sea so I try to go swimming when I'm in Swansea. One morning I went to Langland Bay at 7.30 am – no one about, and I swam out a bit further than usual (I'm no champion swimmer!). Well when I turned to come back, the tide had also turned and after some struggling I found that I was making little or no headway, and I thought, 'I don't think I'm going to make it', and then, 'What if my life is to end here…?' Then I got a bit scared and sent up some arrow prayers, the result of which was that there was an injection of adrenalin and some extra effort and eventually I found myself breathless on the shore! It is not that I would be averse to the Lord saying, 'Come home Ramon' now – indeed it would be a good rounded-off life – but I don't think I want to sink beneath the waves! I'm grateful for the experience, though, and it gives me stimulus to keep on going with great joy and gratitude.

Glasshampton, 22 November 1997

My back and leg pain is still giving me some problems, but it has somewhat abated since six weeks ago when I found it difficult to walk. It is a sign of grace to be able to live positively within limitations, so perhaps I need a bit more grace!

Glasshampton, 18 July 1998

I went on my annual two weeks to Swansea last Saturday, and on Sunday preached at the beautiful small church at Rhosili on the Gower Peninsula – it was packed (I said a *small* church!). The congregation was warm and responsive, and I took off in my usual style of commending our dear Lord as Saviour, Friend and Brother, urging the congregation to do what I have done over my life of Christian pilgrimage – that is to keep a spiritual journal, recording the joys, sorrows and important milestones of life.

On Monday, through the night and into Tuesday I had complete retention of urine, and was admitted as an emergency into Morriston Hospital, Swansea, catheterised, and underwent examination, tests, blood samples, X-ray, etc. They wanted me to stay in to undergo further tests, but when I explained the situation I was discharged on Friday evening with catheter, medication, etc., and told to see my GP with a view to going to the urologist at (probably) Kidderminster Hospital soon.

I returned to Glasshampton yesterday and shall see the GP on Monday, and we shall evaluate what has been done. That is as much as I want to say now, but this letter comes to you so that you may know the situation, and I shall be grateful for your prayers.

I would be glad if you would *not* ring the monastery, otherwise they would be inundated with calls. But if you want further information in about two weeks or so, then let me have a SAE and I shall let you have another letter…

Let us continue to remember one another, for we are all in the Lord's hands, and his love is beyond the measure of our poor thoughts.

(Letter circulated to all his friends) Glasshampton, 16 August 1998

I'm in good heart, and feel enfolded within the love of our Lord. Yesterday Mike Mitton (Acorn Healing Trust) came to celebrate the Eucharist and anoint me during our community mass. It was a good and healing experience, and I look to the Lord for his healing grace.

Even out of all this, there is a joy, a warmth, a love and a compassion which shines through your words. I've always valued your friendship over the last two decades, and was disappointed not to meet up with you this year. I think I may come for a 'quiet' week in Swansea when things are sorted out, and perhaps we can have an hour together then?

I cannot help but believe that the next chapter is going to be a good one, though I may have some limitations...

Glasshampton, 29 August 1998

Let me say straight away that I continue to go forward, free from catheter problems, the former pain gone, and feeling in good heart! I see the spiritual and medical working in concert. The diagnosis of prostate cancer with pelvic spread is not taken lightly! But the anointing/Eucharist with the prayers of God's people, plus the manipulative hormonal therapy are working together in a harmony of therapeutic healing in which our Lord's healing graces are manifest. Do you know that lovely passage in the Apocrypha in Ecclesiasticus 38:1–15 which every doctor should have on his/her surgery wall:

> My child, when you are ill, do not delay, but pray to the Lord, and he will heal you... Give the physician his place, for the Lord created him... for they too pray to the Lord that he will grant them success in diagnosis and in healing, for the sake of preserving life.

This is not a 'double insurance', but an acknowledgement that the Lord is the source of life and healing, and its expression through medicine...

Glasshampton, 31 October 1998

I am writing this after my early morning prayer time and before I get ready to go off to have my third abdominal injected implant of Goseralin hormones. That brings me to say that I continue to quietly progress, and am in good spirit – waterworks okay, pain almost entirely gone – only twinges, energy levels back (I'm winter digging!) and full of joy. So rejoice with me, and continue your prayers.

There is much to share, but I am a bit short of time just now. I wanted, though, to say how much I CONTINUE to value our precious friendship, R. It has continued unabated through the years – we have known each other for *at least* 45 years! I was so glad to see you when you visited lately. That was before I had to take a closer look at my mortality, but I am now aware that the Lord wants me to continue here for a while…

Glasshampton, 16 December 1998

Why am I writing to you today? I'm not altogether sure, but I wonder if you are okay. Perhaps I am so aware of the preciousness and precariousness of the human network down here that I want to keep our friendship in good repair, as if it could be otherwise? I told you that I was going gently forward in my last letter, and I'm glad to report that this continues. We are waterlogged and muddy here, but I've dug and planted four rows of broad beans, symbolic of my new lease of life, and outside my hut I have 18 striped blue crocuses, and daffodils showing the beginnings of their yellow and golden glory. How amazing I find it simply to be here, just to be held within the divine love and yet suffused with the sadness of our world, and these are not incompatible for I believe more than ever that in our Lord's earthly life he constantly felt the mingling of such glory and melancholy in the fullness of his humanity. I do believe that the renewal of the image of God means a recapitulation of the humanity of our Lord Jesus, and then in union with him moving towards the profound mystery of the divine love of the Father – all brought about by the life-giving power of the divine Spirit.

Glasshampton, 2 March 1999

I am having a bit of a 'stony and thorny' path with pelvic pain and limitation of movement, indicating that the disease is still active in the pelvis, and I am having a pelvic X-ray scan at the City Hospital, Birmingham on the 16th, then I shall see the consultant again. I have accepted that I am not to look for some 'instant healing', but that the Lord will give me his healing and enabling power as I live within the limitations of my thorn in the flesh. I am surprised that I am accepting this with such patience (I have my days!), but I do find that lower energy levels and concentration levels are not easy. Yet I continue to rejoice and experience the Lord's blessing on my limited ministry. I am seeing less people now and have just resigned as gardener. Do you remember the quaint AV text 'I cannot dig – to beg I am ashamed' [Luke 16:3]? Well, I don't mind begging, but I can't dig and ride a bike – and both those make me sad. But enough of that or I shall become a hypochondriac. I must say though that the harvest has been good and the greenhouse is still full of lovely red tomatoes.

I think, R, that you are too negative in self-evaluation when you speak of your loss of excitement and joy in preaching. We go through times and phases of ministry in which we are 'required' to lay certain areas aside and enter more deeply into other. When I heard the clear word: 'Be silent or I shall silence you', causing me to take off into solitude in 1990, it was clear to me that I should stop my soap-box ministry. When recently I've refused invitations to preach at the packed sports stadium at Yeovil on Whitsunday and again to 1,000+ at Worcester Cathedral Millennium Celebration concluding the multifaceted day in the cathedral grounds, it is with this sense of 'that kind of ministry is over for you'. I felt a bit of that when you first wrote, years ago, saying that you felt that the 'pastoral ministry' needed to give way to some other form of ministry. You are now growing in the value of silence, solitude and the mystical tradition (which has always been in your soul). Will you read again the chapter 'Guarding the Fire' in *The Flame of Sacred Love,* and I think you will get the taste of what I am saying. There is much more to be said and perhaps we should continue, but I think this book will 'lead you along'. I'm presuming you have it. If not, let me know and I'll get one to you post-haste. Indeed, as I think of some of those who 'can't stop preaching' in their retirement, I wonder if they should look again at the Hindu tradition which counsels that an older man must lay aside his responsibilities and 'go into the forest' to know himself, to face the mystery of Brahman/atman and learn to die. I didn't mean to finish on such a note, but it is appropriate and I greet you in life and joy dear brother…

Glasshampton, 7 September 1999

When I arrived back here, there were 65 pieces of mail waiting. Of course, some of it went into the wastebasket, but I don't want to put your letter at the bottom, so here I am! You will have heard that the latter part of my Swansea trip was not as positive as the first. I went with Ieuan to the 8.00 am Eucharist at All Saints on the last Sunday, against his advice for I had pain and limitation of movement. At 8.15 am, I went suddenly cold, with perspiration running down my face and knew that unless I got out I would faint off. So we returned and in an hour tucked up with a hot water bottle and I was fairly okay again. We were to return the next day, but then Ieuan fell down the stairs bumping spine and ribs so we had to wait until the Tuesday. But I'm on a more even keel now, though still with problems, and on the 16th shall be having an X-ray pelvic scan at City Hospital, Birmingham, then to see the consultant again. But I continue to be aware of our Lord's grace through it all, not expecting any 'instant healing' but realising that I have to live within the 'thorn in the flesh' limitations and trust from day to day. I am a little surprised that I seem to be doing that, though it is not easy to experience lower energy and concentration levels – a new experience! But that's enough of all that lest I become a hypochondriac!

The previous Sunday to the above, I was at All Saints and saw Rowan there in sweater and jeans – visiting his parents. I was so sorry to hear of his mother's death, but realised that it was imminent. As I see how difficult it is for so many with elderly parents, it makes me very grateful that in spite of the hard time my father had during the last few years, I was able to share so much time with him, and the end for them both (within three weeks of each other) was very sad but right. And since then I have been able to feel their nearness within the communion of saints. I intended to visit the grave as I usually do, but was not able to this year because of the events of the last week. How good and precious to have had a good and loving childhood, for it is a firm foundation on which to build an emotionally secure life with a sense of one's worth and love.

I've just read the proofs of my Lent 2000 book for BRF. They tell me that the *Flame* book has sold 3,500 copies and expect the Lent book to do even better. And Ligouri Publications (Missouri, USA) are reprinting my 1990 book *Heaven on Earth* and probably the *Mountain* book. I'll let you know how the sharing goes with Simon Barrington-Ward (26–30 October), for I get the feeling that the results of that will be good. But I also feel that after the present spate of writing I should reconsider my writing ministry. I shall continue with the BRF notes, but perhaps draw in my horns and give the time to being just before the Lord, linked to pacing my intellectual as well as my physical life.

Commending you and M to the loving care of our Lord and looking forward to seeing your friendly faces again. Let us continue to pray for each other, and trust the Lord to bless our ministries with a measure of health and joy.

Glasshampton, 7 September 1999

Since Christmas I have received 200 pieces of mail, most of which has not received direct reply. I want to apologise, but I know you understand that I have been unable to respond owing to lack of energy and concentration. Perhaps this 'round robin' indicates that with this spring has come a renewal of life. You know I am not wanting to make physical or spiritual claims to healing which are not real, and that is why I acknowledge that I have known both dark and healing days and periods over the last year and you have been with me in this. I write now to say that the GP and nursing team feel positive about the result of the medical treatment. The pain team have got that under control, blood counts vary but energy and concentration levels enable me to have good days of joy and creativity. The last few months have yielded a spiritual journey unknown before, both in terms of darkness and light, and though I feel restrained by the Lord to speak about them (for they are in the secret places of his presence, save to my spiritual director friends), they are abundant evidence to me that the dimension of love and prayer is deepening still, and leading me to the place of his healing will. This does not mean any of those slick and quick fixes which I spoke about in my last letter, but are in the realm of the spiritual, and they spill over into the physical...

You will know that I moved up from my hut enclosure around 13 October and the remarkable thing is that I am here in a solitary tower and my solitude is kept as guarded as seems right for the present and can be regulated well. There were secret tears and a sense of bereavement, as you can imagine, for I had worked towards that hut enclosure solitude up to 1990 and had nearly ten years between Tymawr (three years) and Glasshampton since 1993. But there is unexpected joy too, and I so acknowledge that it is a pattern of many hermits through the ages that these periods and episodes take place. As to writing, I have had to tell Lion Books that I cannot fulfil our agreement on the book on St Francis. It had been an enthusiastic project and they have been so gracious in their acceptance of such a decision. Bishop Simon Barrington-Ward spent the inside of a week here during September, and although the pain was not under control at that time, we had an amazing time of profound fellowship in and through the Jesus Prayer each morning. I had wondered if our projected book *Praying the Jesus Prayer Together* was also to be included. But after his recent second visit and a talk with Father Donald Allchin (and prayer all round!), it seems that we should go forward in this, and my GP and team agree. So add this to your prayers. Of course, much of it lies within our hearts and is being written there – but we shall need the effort, concentration and inspiration to get down to the practical production of the book, and

BRF (The Bible Reading Fellowship) are so cooperative too. It seems then that I shall not write to deadline objectives any longer, and this is another small bereavement. I am grateful for the amazingly positive ways I am taking to these, marking the difference that the veteran missionary Amy Carmichael makes between 'resignation' and 'acceptance' – the latter being part of the positive will of God. There is a great deal more I could say, but at least this letter is a 'springtime' one and we can rejoice together and receive our Lord's mutual grace for us both.

Glasshampton, spring 2000

ANTHOLOGY

The following extracts from Ramon's books are arranged in themes. Questions for discussion or reflection for groups or individuals have been added at the end of each section.

Journeying in faith: the pilgrimage

The altar of my heart
from *The Flame of Sacred Love*

'The mean altar of my heart' is the place where real conversion begins. In every human being this altar exists. It is 'mean' not in the sense of narrow, spiteful and skinflint, but in the sense of simple, humble and low. Of course, the human heart may stray from the love and generosity of God, and then it does become mean in the negative sense. Because we live in a fallen world, it is common experience to find that human hearts are often closed to compassion, self-centred in orientation and narrow and exclusive in attitude. This is why conversion is essential and central in any approach to the spiritual life. We all need to be converted, and have an ongoing experience of daily conversion, not just some emotional 'high' that is divorced from the hard disciplines of daily life.

This means that conversion *may* be a 'moment' of dazzling enlightenment, when the sinner is turned from his or her selfish or evil life to the glory of the Sun of Righteousness. This was the case with Saul of Tarsus, and with many great sinners in the story of the church. But it may also be a process of illumination along the way in which formal or dutiful religion is transformed by the light of God's grace when the human heart is touched by the Holy Spirit. Then the religion which was formerly merely a duty or a burden becomes an inexpressible joy which irradiates the whole of life, beginning a pilgrimage which is altogether new.

[*The 'mean altar of my heart' comes from Charles Wesley's hymn 'O thou who camest from above.'*]

Fulfilling the vocation
from *Forty Days and Forty Nights*

I didn't know where it would all lead when I began. The exciting and thrilling love of the Lord was the sprat to catch a mackerel! Indeed, I sometimes feel I would not have begun if I had known then what I know now. But the Lord leads us on in gently ascending paths until our feet begin to tread the higher places. I must admit now that I am afraid, and that perhaps if I knew where it may lead I might again fight shy and draw back. But these feelings coexist with the joy and with the enthusiasm and vision which I have glimpsed in scripture, in the Fathers of the desert, the Celtic monks and the early Franciscan friars. All these, with many others, are part of this wonderful way of prayer and solitude which it is my privilege to share.

God's call into new and unknown dimensions can be scary, but such a call indicates his special love for us, and with the call comes the ability to fulfil the vocation, if we are willing. We must let go of the old ways and venture in faith as he leads us.

Our transient pilgrimage
from *A Month with St Francis*

All the physical beauty and attraction of our mortal frames will one day end in death and dissolution. This was especially true of those early pilgrims who travelled across Europe and slept around those pilgrim arches in Assisi. Life was shorter and more brutal in the 13th century, and the magnificence of the noble buildings in Assisi must have seemed eternal. Yet human mortality and natural catastrophe are part of our transient pilgrimage, and as pilgrim sisters and brothers of St Francis we must seek a more durable and eternal habitation beyond the confines of our earthly lives. We do not, nevertheless, despise earthly beauty, but treasure it more – remembering to seek that city with eternal foundations, whose architect and builder is God (Hebrews 11:10).

The call of Christ
from *A Month with St Francis*

As Francis knelt before the crucifix, he heard a tender and compassionate voice speaking to him: 'Francis, do you not see that my house is falling into ruin? Go and repair it for me.' Trembling and amazed, Francis replied, 'Gladly I will do so, O Lord.' And as he began to obey, he realised that a work which began with building stones and manual labour led to the building up of the lives of men, women and children into the living temple of God, inhabited by the Holy Spirit.

There was a long journey ahead, and this moment of call was only the beginning of his conversion. His true conversion continued throughout his life and into eternity. So it is with us. We may experience a dramatic moment of conversion or an initiating call of the Holy Spirit, but that is only the beginning.

Returning home
from *A Month with St Francis*

The most wonderful thing about a pilgrimage is to return home and find that God was there all the time – hidden in the depths of our heart and among our neighbours. Yet the pilgrimage has been necessary for us to perceive that truth. When I made a pilgrimage to Assisi in 1976, I stayed for the first few days in an ecumenical institute, but it was so full of clacking typewriters and ringing telephones that it was a great relief to put on my backpack, and climb to the Darmstadt site halfway up Mount Subasio. It was there I pitched my tent, and with the pilgrims I found stillness, darkness, gentle camaraderie and a genuine Franciscan warmth around the open fire and under an open sky.

Assisi, and all holy places, are to be cherished in the heart, and if they do carry the heavy sense of the numinous presence of God they will also affirm the more profound reality, which is the Spirit's indwelling in the human heart.

Doorways in and gateways out. But the entrance to genuine spiritual life is Christ himself.

God the Father
from *The Hidden Fire*

I come from a loving and emotionally satisfying home, and the close bonds with both parents continue to this day. But it wasn't a specifically 'religious' home. So up to about ten years of age, my understanding of God was primarily what I felt and knew to be true within myself. During that first formative decade I was often alone, and went wandering and wondering along the coast of the Gower peninsula. I often felt a (sometimes overwhelming) sense of presence, of mystery, what I would later call the 'numinous'. There was a mixture of awe, wonder and yearning in this childhood experience. It was not so much a 'heavenly Father image,' in the sense of my own father's relationship to me. I did appreciate that analogy, but there was a more 'impersonal' sense of mystery than that. Let me illustrate.

One day my father was taking me across a busy thoroughfare. He said something like: 'Now keep hold of my hand tightly, because if you don't, you are likely to get run over.' I knew he was not serious in his seriousness. Of course, I was to hold tightly to him, but I also knew that whether I held on or not, he would hold me. There was danger, but with him there I was kept from it by his love and strength. The impersonal nature of the mystery I had felt in the created order was not less than that – but more. It was not that my experience was of the sub-personal, but of the supra-personal…

So it was, in my pilgrimage of prayer, that my early childhood was filled with the sense of the presence of God the Father.

Metanoia: a change of heart
from *Franciscan Spirituality*

In his teaching and example to the friars, Francis showed himself particularly aware of the sophisticated and evasive complications by which we sinners avoid radical confrontation with the holiness of God. He would smell out insincerity and hypocrisy in pseudo-hermits who kept silence because they didn't want to be found out, in friars-to-be who were inflated with their own egocentric desires, or in friars who were lazy and gluttonous, whom he sent on their way.

In this purging or pruning, there is certain to be searing pain involved, and most of us shrink from it and evade facing the surgery. But the next tribulation, catastrophic illness, bereavement or circumstance throws us on to God in complete helplessness, so that he uses even these things to lead us from purgation into illumination.

Yet there is also joy in repentance, and the New Testament word for it is *metanoia,* which means to 'change your heart' rather than 'do penance'. God is not an irritable old man in the sky, hurling thunderbolts of despotic anger on the earth, nor an exacting tyrant who demands retribution. He is rather the yearning father who rejoices when his son or daughter returns home to his embrace. The joy is felt even when the Holy Spirit burns and sears the believer in the purifying crucible of divine love.

Suffering with God
from *Forty Days and Forty Nights*

Struggling and suffering was part of the pilgrimage of Jesus, for his path to glory carried him through the *Via Dolorosa* – the Way of Sorrows. The call to discipleship is no easy option, for the disciple can only tread in the steps of the Master, and the only real discipleship involves the believer in struggle and pain. But this is not negative or destructive suffering – it is creative, redemptive and even joyful.

There is no suffering we can encounter that Jesus has not experienced before us, and no depths that he has not plumbed. Wherever human beings are lonely, imprisoned, tortured, hungry, thirsty, dispossessed or dying – there Jesus suffers too – and there Jesus redeems human suffering.

In Jesus, suffering touches the heart of God, and Jesus' tears are the weeping of the Almighty. God became part of our suffering in order that we may become sharers of his glory. If our suffering participates in the groaning and birth pangs of travail described in the eighth chapter of Romans, then we shall be caught up into the glory and splendour of a new creation in which all suffering will be redeemed and transfigured. For 'I consider that our present sufferings are not worth comparing with the glory that will be revealed in us' (Romans 8:18, NIV).

Keeping a journal
from *Forty Days and Forty Nights*

The recording of one's spiritual quest and pilgrimage, the marking of milestones, the recalling and recording of days of emptiness or splendour – all these can serve to deepen one's relationship with God in prayer and love. Such a task is like the sharing of love letters. The dimensions of the loved one's mind and heart are opened up to you, as yours are opened up to him or her. This is both a discipline and a joy, for you soon find yourself in dialogue with God as well as with your own soul. Not only will you find yourself writing truthfully about yourself at a depth unknown previously, but you will find an almost prophetic emergence of the will of God for your life as it unfolds before you in your journal. And even if this is not transparently evident, you will certainly find that the answers to some of your deepest emotional and spiritual difficulties will be implicit in the way you state the problem.

The return of the prodigal son
from *The Way of Love*

I remembered how moved I was when reading Henri Nouwen's book *The Return of the Prodigal Son,* in which he expounds upon Rembrandt's beautiful painting and the parable. He described how God dealt with him, showing him to be pictured in each of the characters in this amazing parable of Jesus. Every movement in the story stirs up the depths of my own life – the way in which I have grieved the heart of love – in my fellow human beings and in my compassionate Father...

The prodigal son begged for penance and penalty, but the father knew he had drained the dregs of shame, helplessness, frustration and sorrow. The boy hoped for mercy, but was overwhelmed by love. The father was not testing him by waiting. He waited because he would not, could not, force his love. The father waited, yearned, wept, gazed along the road – and as soon as he saw his son 'still far off' his compassion burst into flame, and he ran, ran along the road. The Greek text says *kataphileo* – he kissed him tenderly, endearingly, affectionately. The narrative is alive with excitement, and portrays the old man seeing, pitying, running, falling, kissing and embracing his dear, penitent son.

The boy is overwhelmed and stumbles over his confession, pouring out his sorrow, pleading forgiveness. As I look at Rembrandt's beautiful painting and see the bedraggled, dirty, weary, helpless son, on his knees with his head buried in the bosom of the embracing father, I can hear him say, 'My son, my son... I don't care where you've been, what you've done, how far you've wandered – today you're home, you're in my arms, and you're mine!' Mother Julian understands:

> *In his love he clothes us,*
> *Enfolds and embraces us;*
> *That tender love completely surrounds us,*
> *Never to leave us.*

Your burning bush
from *The Prayer Mountain*

It was not a *burning bush* that was the means of Brother Lawrence's conversion at 18 years of age, but a tree putting forth its buds in the springtime. He was confronted, amazed and converted! For him, this was God's place and time, and from that simple meeting with God in nature he lived 'practising the presence of God' and died a lay brother in the Order of Discalced Carmelites in Paris at the age of 80.

Your life story may be different from that of Moses or Brother Lawrence, but the pattern is the same, and it is repeated at different points and various levels in your life. Sometimes the sense of awe and wonder is the primary thing; at other times, it is a deep sense of penitence, or a feeling of such passivity that all you can do is to remain in a state of receptivity, allowing God not only to give you strength to stand upon your feet (Daniel 10:9–19), but also to provide the dynamic that will fire and enthuse you in carrying out your vocation and commission.

Questions for reflection or discussion

1 Ramon writes, 'Conversion is essential and central in any approach to the spiritual life.' How would you define 'conversion'? (See 'The altar of my heart', p. 114.)
2 Can you think of particular ways in which God has led you in the choices you have made in the past? (See 'Fulfilling the vocation', p. 115.)
3 Ramon says that, from early childhood, his pilgrimage of prayer was filled with the sense of God as the Father. Do you think of yourself as being a 'child of God' with a heavenly Father? What difference does this make to your relationship with God? (See 'God the Father', p. 117.)
4 Do you think that keeping a spiritual journal would be of value to you on your pilgrimage of faith? (See 'Keeping a journal', p. 119.)

5 Read Luke 15:11–32. Do you think that a better title for the parable rather than 'The return of the prodigal son' is 'The love of the compassionate father'? (See 'The return of the prodigal son', p. 120.)

Praying and reflecting: meditation

The sign of redemption
from *My Questions, God's Questions*

In my hermitage, above the altar-table, I have a large mounted reproduction of the San Damiano crucifix which spoke to St Francis in the early twelfth century... The face of Christ is tender and compassionate, and painted around the cross are 27 smaller figures. Immediately above the head of the crucified Christ is the risen Christ facing ten disciples in glory (Judas is missing). Immediately at the right (wounded) side of Christ are Mary, his mother, and the disciple, John. On the other side are Mary Magdalene and Mary the wife of Cleopas, and the centurion with two soldiers. Above them, either side of the outstretched arms, are six angels, and below his feet are two dim figures which may be Adam and Eve or two Old Testament saints.

The beauty of all this is that the crucified Christ is also the risen Christ, for his arms are outstretched to save, and the whole company of the redeemed surround the cross, with the angelic company – representing the communion of saints in glory.

This is how the cross is to be understood, not as an instrument of torture and execution, but as the tree of life, and the thorn-crowned Saviour is the King of Glory reigning from his throne.

One of the loveliest crucifixes, which I lived with for five years, is the large *Christus Rex* figure over the side altar at St Mary's Episcopal Cathedral, Glasgow. The Christ is robed as priest and king, and although he is lifted up on the cross, he is at the same time triumphant and the reigning one. This, and the San Damiano crucifix, remind us of the One who said, 'Do not be afraid; I am the first and the last, and the living one. I was dead, and see, I am alive forever and ever, and have the keys of Death and of Hades' (Revelation 1:17–18).

Thoughts on meditation
from *Deeper into God*

Meditation on scripture is not teaching or Bible study, and, though you may have a devotional commentary with you, it is naked exposure to scripture that must be involved, not second opinion upon the letter of scripture.

When a lover receives a letter from his loved one, he does not seek other people's opinions about it; he does not approach it in a coldly objective or academic manner; he does not analyse it as to etymological origins, grammatical structure or syntactical techniques. He is not interested in grammar and syntax at the moment, but in his beloved! He will savour the letter, read it slowly, carefully, tenderly. He will reread it, not only the words it says, but its inner and hidden meanings, discoverable only to him. He will thrill to the feel of it, the smell, the touch and texture of it – not because of the paper or odour or ink, but because of the touch and scent and presence of the beloved in it. He will feel, though others may not, the vibrations set up within himself by the letter, and he will understand, interpret and even place it within his shirt and near to his heart. All this is nonsense to the investigator, who will carry out quite other examinations upon the letter, in terms of literary criticism, bringing to bear all the conceptual paraphernalia of critical method…

The purpose of the letter is to mediate the presence of the beloved. And meditation of scripture is also to that end. With this difference – the letter can only mediate, communicate, revitalise in the *absence* of the beloved. What purpose would the letter serve if the beloved was herself present?… She would say: 'What are you doing? Lay the letter aside, for I am here before you – delight in *me,* and take me to yourself, for I love you!'

Praying the Jesus Prayer
from *Praying the Jesus Prayer Together*

If you persevere with the Jesus Prayer, it will root itself within your heart by the power of the Holy Spirit and a gentle flame will begin to burn, a bubbling spring will arise and you will actually find that the apostolic injunction 'Pray without ceasing' will become part of your life. When you wake in the morning, the prayer will echo in your being; as you go about your daily work, the quiet flame will be burning; as you relate to people and situations, the spring will be bubbling; as you enter into the resolution of conflicts, meet problems, encounter difficulties… as you live in love and truth and spread hope around, the power of the prayer will energise you, and as you go to bed at night, the mighty name of Jesus will guard and keep you. Through the dark hours of the night, when you wake in the stillness, the holy name of Jesus will refresh you, and as you commend yourself again to sleep, the name of Jesus will refresh you. This is why one Orthodox monk said that when he discovered the Jesus Prayer, he felt like the man in the Gospel who had found the pearl of greatest price…

The second great commandment of Jesus is, 'You shall love your neighbour as yourself.' It is the one whose heart is aflame with the love of Jesus who can effectively radiate compassion and stretch out a hand in practical help to those in need.

[The Jesus Prayer: 'Jesus, son of the living God, have mercy on me, a sinner.']

The hidden life
from *Deeper into God*

It is in the life of Jesus, *par excellence,* that we become aware of the hidden dimension of the life of contemplative prayer. There are constant references to holy places, spending all night in prayer, hours of sacred tryst with the Father on the mountain. But quite apart from all these periods of physical withdrawal and retreat, there is the awareness of the fact that Jesus carried with him an interior stillness, and a dimension of contemplation in which he was continually living, walking, moving in the Holy Spirit. The Spirit was given to him without measure, and he did and said those things which continually manifested and glorified the Father. And all this because he lived and matured over the years of young manhood in the school of obedience and prayer.

Alive for evermore
from *Forty Days and Forty Nights*

The stone had been rolled across the entrance to the tomb. Pilate's seal was set and the soldiers kept their watch. It seemed to the disciples and to the world at large that you had become a prisoner in the kingdom of the dead. It had finally come to an end.

But life began to stir within the tomb before the rising of the sun. The pure light of the Holy Spirit began to shine and your body, Lord Jesus, loosed from its imprisoning bands of myrrh and ointments and came forth in risen glory. The boundless energy of your new and immortal life burst the bands of death, rolled the stone away, blinded the soldiers and greeted the lesser sun of creation in its rising.

We remember today all the sorrows of Calvary, and feel the grief in our own hearts. But we look for the empty tomb, the glorious rising, eternal life as a present gift and grace and the life of the world to come.

'I AM he who lives and was dead,' says the Lord, 'and behold I am alive for evermore, and have the keys of hell and death...'

A hidden fire
from *A Hidden Fire*

It isn't easy to keep a fire hidden, and it is the paradox of the fire of God that it is both hidden and manifest. The fire which burned upon the holy altar of God was never to be extinguished: 'Fire shall be kept burning on the altar continually; it shall not go out' (Leviticus 6:13, ESV). It symbolises the fire of the divine love and the divine holiness of which Charles Wesley writes:

O Thou who camest from above
The pure celestial fire to impart,
Kindle a flame of sacred love
On the mean altar of my heart.

It is a fire that belongs to God. It burns upon God's altar in his most holy temple. We are the temple of God, and our inmost heart is the altar of the living God. As John Chrysostom says, 'No matter where we happen to be, by prayer we set up an altar to God in our hearts.' James Montgomery speaks of this hiddenness in his hymn on the many aspects of prayer:

Prayer is the soul's sincere desire,
Uttered or unexpressed;
The motion of a hidden fire
That trembles in the breast.

The radiance of God
from *The Flame of Sacred Love*

The New Testament is full of the light and glory of spiritual experience, and Paul writes a marvellous chapter about the Holy Spirit as the outshining radiance of God in the second letter to the Corinthians. After speaking of the fading light and glory of the holy covenant reflected on the face of Moses, he says that the Spirit of God shines with gospel light upon us, and we reflect back that glory, while we are being transformed from one degree of glory to another (2 Corinthians 3:18). Then he links the Spirit's light which shone in the darkness and chaos at creation with the gospel light which illumines the heart of the believer:

For it is the God who said, 'Let light shine out of darkness', who has shone in our hearts to give the light of the knowledge of the glory of God in the face of Jesus Christ.

2 CORINTHIANS 4:6

Intercession: a network of compassion
from *My Questions, God's Questions*

Some Christians question the very possibility of petitionary and intercessory prayer and, after years of 'shopping-list prayer', give up because they are not persuaded of its efficacy and question its theology.

Prayer is communion with God, and this is much wider and deeper than petition or intercession. Through my writings, I have spent many years in leading Evangelical and Catholic Christians into the profound wonder and mystery of contemplative prayer. But I do not therefore neglect prayers of petition or intercession – though I now understand them in a different way.

When I ask people to pray for or with me, or when people ask me to pray for them, I enter into a network of compassion. I yield myself to God in order that the Holy Spirit may groan and cry, weep and worship in and through me – expressing the healing will of God. It is as though I were the flute through which the Holy Spirit breathes, creating melodies of intercession.

The saving, reconciling energies of God flow along this creative network of compassion, communicating healing love among warring nations, deprived and tortured people, and bringing hope into the lives of helpless, terminally ill folk. These energies work towards the alleviation of suffering, towards deliverance, or a good and gentle death.

So no prayer is individualistic, though it may be intensely personal. We are all in it together, and our prayer is the prayer of the cosmic Christ. All true prayer is offered within the communion of saints. If it is 'in the Spirit' (that is, linked with this network of compassion), then it contributes towards an increase of hope, light and love in the world.

So, if prayer is viewed in this cosmic manner and as part of the ongoing prayer of Christ to the Father, it becomes universal, part of the whole contemplative venture, and is one with the healing energies of God in nature and within humanity as a whole.

So, get thinking, get praying at a more profound level, and with all the saints!

When you feel the absence of God
from *The Heart of Prayer*

A person who has known and loved God in Christ over a number of years, and has rejoiced in sacramental gifts and graces, may find the life of meditative and intercessory prayer drying up, a loss of vision and enthusiasm for evangelistic and pastoral ministry, and a withdrawal and absence of the sense of God's loving, guiding and joyful presence...

I used to be scared of deep water, and if I found myself just out of my depth at sea I would struggle and flail around in a combination of breast and over-arm stroke until I could feel the firm sand beneath my feet again. I learned eventually that it was better to lie on my back, float freely and affect some rhythmic back strokes. So in this situation, when God is at work, simply float, be still, gentle, quiet, passive – let him do what he wants. Then you will find that this attitude itself becomes a pattern of prayer.

Practising prayer
from *A Hidden Fire*

It is certain that unless a pianist gives time and space to practice, he will not truly play; unless a writer saturates himself with literature, he will not truly write; unless a potter gives hand and heart to his clay, he will not truly centre; unless a lover gives himself body and soul to his beloved, he will not truly love. So what does this say about prayer and God?

Time for God
from *A Hidden Fire*

Within the time-flow of quantitative time, God calls us to qualitative times of decision, of renewal, of confrontation, of prayer, leading to deeper union with himself. These are God's moments, and when they occur we must be ready. Time for God is a prime necessity and a priority in our lives.

Jesus was aware that his coming was in fulfilment of the divine *kairos,* and he felt his time, his hour of passion and glory drawing near (Mark 1:5; Matthew 26:18). So there are moments of *kairos* in our lives when discovery, enlightenment and challenge confront and invade us. Time is a precious commodity in our world. 'I haven't got time – I'm too busy' is heard on every hand, and there is no time to 'waste'. But if you are too busy for God, then you are just too busy! I've never met anyone who possesses a TV set who had no time to view! We need to waste time with God as we would waste time on a loved one – not doing or planning or thinking, but simply *being* in his presence and resting in his love. We cannot dictate to God the time or manner of his revelation to us, for he is free and sovereign, and his *kairos* is dependent upon his own loving will. Yet he calls upon us to wait on him, to gaze upon his glory, to spend time prodigiously, so that we are open and receptive to the *kairos* of his revelation to us (Isaiah 40:31; 2 Timothy 4:6).[73]

Taken into the life of the Trinity
from *A Hidden Fire*

The risen and glorified Christ ascended to where he was before, in full communion and being with the Father and the Spirit, within the interpenetration of the divine life (John 6:62). We, as individual believers and members of the body of Christ, are drawn into actual participation in the life of the Holy Trinity. The Greek Fathers, following the mystical teaching of the New Testament, use the term *theosis* ('divinisation') for such mystical sharing (John 17:20–26). They mean, by this, not an impersonal pantheism, but a true sharing of the divine life, in which our isolation and individualism is overcome and caught up into the fullness and fountainhead of the Personal, finding our true identity in God, Father, Son and Holy Spirit.

The lover and the beloved
from *A Hidden Fire*

When the lover receives a letter from the beloved, or looks upon her photographs or a gift she has given him, he will meditate upon her loveliness. He will not only recall the qualities which reflect the beauty of her mind and body, but upon the very nature of her being, that mingling of their lives in which the wellspring of love bubbles up to the mutual delight of one another.

To meditate upon the qualities of the beloved brings one to the borderland of mystical prayer where scripture, mystical theology, devotional classics, hymnology, poetry, the beauty of the created order and the whole gamut of positive human relations remind one of the Beloved. Ramon Lull, the 13th-century Franciscan, in his *Book of the Lover and the Beloved,* is carried away by such an analogy:

> The Lover went in desire of his Beloved, and he met two friends who greeted and embraced and kissed each other with love and tears. And the Lover swooned, so strongly did these two lovers call his Beloved to mind.[74]

The devotional classics of both the Catholic and Evangelical traditions are full of the mutual love which indwells the believer and his Lord, drawing deeply on the analogy of human love. St Bernard's sermons on the Song of Songs are an extended meditation on the loveliness of God in Christ, and the poetry of St John of the Cross catches the experiential wonder of the soul caught up in meditative adoration of the Beloved. Meditation in the light of the Holy Spirit stimulates yearning in the heart of the believer. On the pattern and analogy of human love, meditative prayer in love leads to yearning for union with the Beloved.

The transfiguration
from *A Hidden Fire*

In the account of the transfiguration, we have the life of prayer portrayed before our very eyes. The initiative is with the Father; Jesus gives himself to the prayer of vision in self-surrendered freedom and discipline; the uncreated light of the Holy Spirit floods his being and overflows into the natural order. Here is not only a penetration into the mystery of God, but an awareness of the communion of saints, the shared experience of saints on earth and in heaven. The divine presence saturates the mountain, and the voice from the excellent glory fills the disciples with awe and amazement (2 Peter 1:16–18).

These are moments of wonder, of holy fear, of contemplative vision. The plain of human need stretches out below with all its opportunities and challenges to loving service. But here on the holy mount, the vision encapsulates and saturates all those caught up in its glory.

Jesus carries the glory from the mount to the plain. The splendour and vision of the glory of God is translated into compassion, healing and works of mercy. Jesus, humble and transfigured, is the paradigm of the life of prayer. And we are called to follow him.

Remembering
from *Forty Days and Forty Nights*

'Remember me' is an arrow prayer which arises from a longing heart. Hannah prays this prayer as she longs for a child (1 Samuel 1:11); Joseph prays it, incarcerated unjustly in prison (Genesis 40:14); Samson prays it in his blindness and weakness after he has been taunted as a fool (Judges 16:28). Jeremiah prays it as his enemies close in to destroy him (Jeremiah 15:15); Hezekiah prays it after the sentence of death, crying for reprieve (2 Kings 20:3).

All these prayers are heard and answered. Perhaps the penitent thief who was crucified with Jesus had heard these stories from his childhood, for when the impenitent thief taunted Jesus he rebuked him, and, turning in his dying agony to the crucified Saviour, he prayed the same prayer which had sounded down through Jewish history and was answered by the God who receives the penitent and forgives: 'Jesus, remember me when you come into your kingdom.' Jesus answered him, 'Truly, today you will be with me in paradise' [Luke 23:42–43].

Memory is so alive for me that I often take a memory walk as a way of praying. I go walking in a quiet place and select a memory from my rich tapestry of experience and talk it through with the Lord. It may be a precious memory of my parents or loved ones in which great joy and some rich humour is uppermost. Or it may be a sad memory of failure, broken relationships, a misunderstanding or bitter words spoken in a reactionary moment and ever since regretted.

Travelling through the memory, I speak in the present to those who inhabit the memory with me – affirming love, confessing sorrow or righting moments, words and experiences which have gone awry. And because this is done in the presence of the Lord, he pours his blessing and healing into the memories and puts right things beyond my power to change.

Lord Jesus, Son of the living God
from *Praying the Jesus Prayer Together*

'*Let your healing flow down upon me*': This is directed to Christ as *Pantocrator* – the transcendent Christ who gazes into the believer's heart, as depicted in paintings on the dome of an Orthodox church or icon. We may also contemplate the ever-deepening love flowing from the Father's heart, carrying life and fertility wherever it flows. We ask that this transcendent blessing, the cleansing river, may flow over and into us, bringing healing, life and peace.

'*Let your healing spring up within me*': God's Holy Spirit dwells within us, and our bodies are the temples of the Spirit, awaiting the rising springs of restorative powers that already reside within. This plea is directed towards the immanent Christ – the interior, indwelling mystery of Christ within, the 'hope of glory' (Colossians 1:27). The image is of a bubbling spring of healing water, a gentle, murmuring stream which, when the rubble is cleared, will spring up into every crevice of our being: 'Out of the believer's heart shall flow rivers of living water' (John 7:38).

'*Let your healing love enfold me*': If Christ is transcendent *above* us and immanent *within* us, he also completely surrounds us, caressing and holding us within himself, like protected children within the embrace of their mother. This is not a regress to the protecting womb for fear of the wicked world, but a retreat into the divine love so that, sustained and restored, we may return to the world as witnesses to God's embrace.

'*Let your healing power flow through me*': God's healing power does not stagnate in an interior lake with no outlet. Love always flows, and we are channels of its communication. If we experience the forgiving, healing and peace of God, then we shall become channels of blessing to others. The indwelling Spirit will flow through us and affect those around us, either physically or through prayers, joy and compassion.

Mary at the cross
from *The Prayer Mountain*

In my hut chapel, I have a large reproduction of the crucifix that spoke to St Francis at the church of St Damiano and that was the stimulus to his conversion. On the right of the Saviour stand Mary and John beneath his wounded side, the water symbolising our baptism, and the blood symbolising his cleansing power and the Eucharist.

The mighty task which Christ was accomplishing in his passion and death was the work of our salvation, and we have already been aware of the powerful things which were taking place on Mount Calvary. But right in the midst of it, when her dear Son was hanging in pain and desolation, there drew near Mary his mother, with John the disciple and that faithful group of women. The 13th-century hymn, thought to be from the hand of Jacopone da Todu, begins:

At the Cross her station keeping,
Stood the mournful Mother weeping,
Close to Jesus at the last.
Through her soul, of joy bereavèd,
Bowed with anguish, deeply grievèd,
Now at length the sword has passed.

As they stood in silent sorrow at the cross, Mary and John were held within the circle of Calvary love. Jesus gave them both into one another's keeping, and this is John the evangelist's way of drawing us into this circle of loving communion as we share the sorrow of our Saviour's death.

Then we may identify ourselves with John the disciple, loving Jesus to the end, and feel our intimate affinity with Mary as the mother-figure of the church. Not only do we give reverence and honour to Mary as the mother of our Lord, but in her we see that we are not separate believers, but a part of the communion of saints and of the eucharistic fellowship, members of the body of Christ.

At the foot of the cross, we enter into the pain and sorrow of Mary and John, and as our tears mingle with theirs, in the very fellowship of grief we find some relief and even a ray of hope.

The joy of the cross
from *Fullness of Joy*

We cannot understand the darkness and terror of the cross to Jesus. The Garden of Gethsemane is an indication of the profound depths of spiritual agony which our Lord endured in anticipation of the bleak hill of Golgotha, the place of the skull. The strange cry of dereliction sounds through the desolate darkness and down through the ages, re-echoed in every human cry of pain: 'My God, my God, why have you forsaken me?' The sun is veiled and the earth quakes at that cry, and nature shudders at its sound. This reveals to us the manner in which God himself is involved in the pain and sorrow of our humanity, not merely having compassion from afar, but incarnating himself in human flesh in order that he might descend into the depths of human sin, pain and alienation.

But there is another side to it. Looking back on the path that Jesus trod, the theology of the epistle to the Hebrews portrays him as entering into the joy of the redeemed even as he descended into the abyss of darkness and death. He not only endured the cross, but gloried in it:

> Jesus the pioneer and perfecter of our faith, who for the joy that was set before him endured the cross, despising the shame, and is seated at the right hand of the throne of God.
>
> HEBREWS 12:2, RSV

This was no superficial or transient joy for the Man of Sorrows who was acquainted with grief. But it was the joy of consummation – the prodigal son had returned to the Father, the wandering sheep was brought back to the true fold by the Good Shepherd.

Joy comes in the morning
from *Fullness of Joy*

The empty tomb is not a matter for speculation but for celebration, and the fact that Jesus was no longer in the tomb means not only that he is 'existentially' present within the heart, but that he will bring to an end the present historical process at his coming in glory. He will initiate the kingdom of God in *eschatological* (end-of-the-world) destruction and transfiguration, putting an end to evil and death. The temporal process, as we know it, will be no more, and all the prophetic promises of scripture, at present clothed in analogy, metaphor and parable, will be caught up in unimaginable wonder and ineffable glory...

The stories of the transfiguration and resurrection are the basis for our hope, reflected in one of the loveliest promises of the New Testament contained in the epistle to the Philippians:

> Our commonwealth is in heaven, and from it we await a Saviour, the Lord Jesus Christ, who will change our lowly body to be like his glorious body, by the power which enables him even to subject all things to himself.
> PHILIPPIANS 3:20–21, RSV

So the theme of joy has been the golden thread throughout creation, redemption and consummation. The fullness of such joy is not yet. We have the foretaste, pledge, promise, hope, but the fullness yet awaits us. The anticipation of joy in God forever gives me joy at the present moment. My ecstasies and despairs in this mortal state are all bound up in such anticipation, and the restlessness of heart which I now experience is akin to the patient and impatient attitude of the lover who awaits the coming of the Beloved.

In this poor world, we live in the darkness before dawn. We are assured that though the weeping may endure for a night, joy comes in the morning, and already the wide sky is heavy with anticipation and expectant longing, so that the last words of the Bible are entirely appropriate:

> He who testifies to these things says, 'Surely I am coming soon.' Amen. Come, Lord Jesus! The grace of the Lord Jesus be with all the saints. Amen.
> REVELATION 22:20, ESV

The inspiration of scripture
from *The Flame of Sacred Love*

The word 'inspiration' is rare. It occurs only once in the New Testament, though it is a powerful analogy and its implications are found through the whole Bible. The basic text is 2 Timothy 3:16–17:

> All scripture is inspired [*theopneustos*] by God and is useful for teaching, for reproof, for correction, and for training in righteousness, so that everyone who belongs to God may be proficient, equipped for every good work.

Literally, the word 'inspired', *theopneustos,* means 'God-breathed', and it immediately brings to mind the picture of God breathing into Adam the breath of life, so that he became a living being (Genesis 2:7). The breath of God is the Holy Spirit, for the Hebrew word *rauch* and the Greek word *pneuma* both mean spirit, wind or breath, in the Bible. The breath of God is universal, breathing life and fertility throughout the natural order, sustaining animate life in all sentient beings, and inspiring all that is creative, good and true in human endeavour.

This Holy Spirit breathes in creation and redemption, moving the sinner to repentance, communicating the powers of the new birth, and inspiring the human heart at all levels, and especially through the prophetic word of scripture.

Questions for reflection or discussion

1 Reflect on Ramon's perception of the cross 'as the tree of life, and the thorn-crowned Saviour as the King of Glory reigning from the throne'. Do you find this concept helpful as you think of the cross as a sign of redemption? (See 'The sign of redemption', p. 123.)

2 How can repetition of the Jesus Prayer reflect Paul's urging to 'pray in the Spirit at all times in every prayer and supplication' (Ephesians 6:18) and to 'pray without ceasing' (1 Thessalonians 5:17)? (See 'Praying the Jesus Prayer', p. 125.)

3 Read and ponder on 2 Corinthians 3:18. In what ways can we conceive of God as a living, personal presence? (See 'The radiance of God', p. 127.)

4 Spend some time meditating on the story of the transfiguration of Jesus (Luke 9:28–36). What is God saying to you in this event? What do you want to say to God? (See 'The transfiguration', p. 132.)

5 Ramon writes, 'The Holy Spirit breathes in creation and redemption moving sinners to repentance, communicating the power of new birth, and inspiring human hearts at all levels, and especially through the prophetic word of scripture'. Reflect on these words and their meaning for you. (See 'The inspiration of scripture', p. 138.)

Alone with God: solitude

The cell within
from *A Month with St Francis*

I live in a wooden hut, in an enclosure in the grounds of Glasshampton monastery, Worcester; and I have friends who have erected simple meditation huts in their gardens. But Francis gets to the root of the matter:

> Everyone has a cell – their body. Every man, woman and child should treat their body with reverence and simplicity, not pampering it, but not [as he later realised] being cruel to it. The person who inhabits that cell of the body must live in creative joy, in praying and singing, and in praise of God. This positive life will overflow, bringing love, hope and peace to others.

A limited number of people come to my wooden hut, and they find such warmth inside that we are comforted together in the fellowship of our elder brother Francis, and most of all in the forgiveness and love of our greater brother and Saviour, Jesus. This is the basis of universal compassion and relationship with the whole creation.

Confronting the living God
from *Forty Days and Forty Nights*

The cave, in the mystical tradition, is the depth of the human heart which may become the cave of God's indwelling. It is a terrifying and yet an assuring place. Terrifying, because you have to face the stripped and naked self which you become when confronted by the divine mystery of God's holiness and love; assuring, because, with all its dark mystery, it is the covenanted trysting place where the soul rests in the bosom of God.

One of the primary things that solitude teaches me is to tremble in God's presence. Living close to nature in surroundings exposing me to the change of seasons in hermit solitude causes a trembling born of both joy and reverential awe. The Desert Fathers espoused no sentimental concept of an easy-going God, nor any philosophical view of a divine Absolute. They were confronted with the living God of scripture and desert before whom they fell down in fear and trembling.

I am not a nature mystic or a sentimental animal-lover roving around springtime fields and woods, penning verses and indulging in vague general benevolence for the human race while absenting myself from my fellow human beings and from the hurry and grime of the marketplace. I live in fear and trembling because of God's holy love and because of his loving holiness.

The desert of the heart
from *Forty Days and Forty Nights*

For everyone, there is a call into the desert. But few truly respond to that call. Some fail to hear it because their lives are cluttered with schemes, possessions and ambitions which drown the call of the Spirit. Even those who hear the call may then close their ears because they are afraid of facing God in the nakedness of solitude, or because they suspect that God will challenge them with the demands of the divine love. Those who hear and feel an answering yearning deep within their own hearts may be tempted and deflected by the claims of family, career or a society which places before the believer the insistent duties of what seems to be the 'real world'.

But there are some who hear the call clearly, who free themselves from sins, worldly attachments and lesser loves to follow the call into the desert for a confrontation with the living God.

The desert may be a geographical location where the man or woman waits in solitude; it may be a state of mind which is open to new guidance and revelation; it will certainly be a desert of the heart which is the trysting-place where God meets with those who long for him.

Listen then for that call, which is ever sounding. When its echo reverberates in your heart, give yourself to it in love, for in surrendering to the call of the desert you will be enveloped in that mystery for which you were made – union with the living God.

Dwelling *within* him
from *A Hidden Fire*

The indwelling rest which is found in the Lord is a rest from the weight and burden of our sins, and a refuge in time of tribulation and persecution. But primarily and ultimately, it is an interior resting in his love. It is the child resting on the breast of its mother (Psalm 131:2), the lover resting in the beloved (Song of Songs 7:1–10). One of the stanzas of F.W. Faber's hymn on the majesty of God is criticised because it is misunderstood, but it carries this feeling of wonder and contemplative resting:

> *Father of Jesus, love's reward*
> *What rapture shall it be,*
> *Prostrate before thy throne to lie*
> *And gaze, and gaze on thee?*

There are times when such an experience comes after long hours of waiting in darkness, yearning for a revelation of the tenderness of Christ. St John of the Cross portrays the soul as wounded by the love of Christ in conversion and the beginnings of contemplative prayer and comments:

> The healing of the wounds of love comes only from him who inflicted the wounds. Hence the soul says that she went forth calling for him who dealt with the wound, begging to be healed, crying out at the violence of the burning caused by the wound.

… There are times when the love of God suddenly takes hold of the believer without any particular preparation on the believer's part. It is the surprise of the lover who suddenly approaches and catches away his beloved, and causes her to rest in him, so that they enjoy profound mutual indwelling.

Face to face with God
from *Deeper into God*

Although God told Moses that no man would be able to look upon the divine face and live, yet Moses is spoken of as the patriarch who spoke with God face-to-face. And this divine communication and communion took place primarily in the desert and upon the holy mountain. The biblical roots of retreat are found in such experiences as this in the holy men of old. Only in such places of solitude and retreat could exposure to God at such a level take place, and only in such confrontation and communion could Moses receive the transfiguring power and interior strength to lead the people of God out of slavery into freedom and the land of liberty… St Seraphim writes, 'Acquire inward peace and thousands around you will find their salvation.' Certainly, if Moses had not obeyed the inward prompting of the Holy Spirit to retreat into the desert or up the mountain height, he would never have been the instrument of God's revelation to his ancient people and to the world.

Why retreat?
from *Deeper into God*

Don't be discouraged if you feel that your experience of retreat cannot attain to such high motives as the 'love of God alone'. Loving service, renewal, refreshment and growth in discipleship may be humbler motives, but it is not up to us to define motivation too clearly. The first shall be last and the last first, and those who think their feet to be planted on the high road of holiness may be deluded. And those who feel that they are on the lowly path of humble service may truly be just beneath the summit of the mount. 'Let anyone who thinks that he stands take heed lest he fall' (1 Corinthians 10:12, ESV).

So if you feel the gentle constraint of love to move into retreat, that's alright. But, if you feel driven by circumstances, drawn by longing, encouraged by weakness or even moved by sanctified curiosity, that's alright too. There are many reasons for movement into retreat.

Belonging together
from *The Heart of Prayer*

I do not encourage people to become hermits, but to live an ordinary life of reciprocal love in the world. But I am here for you in order to pray *for* you in the context of the church and the world, and in order to pray *with* you to help you take up the offered disciplines of the spiritual life as they speak to your condition.

You and I are members of the body of Christ, and our vocations may have carried us in different directions, but we belong together. Some of the people who come to see me live most busy and demanding lives, and if they did not develop a contemplative oasis in the midst of it they would go under. Different members of the body have different functions and ministries, and that is how it should be. But all of us must learn to pray, to love, to share and to reflect more and more the glory, the enthusiasm and the compassion of the God who calls us into an ever deepening and intimate fellowship with himself.

Introduction to contemplative life
from *A Hidden Fire*

As I read more of the tradition and learned of the depth in prayer and solitude, several things became clear. I realised that scripture and psalms were the life blood of such contemplative men and women, and necessarily so, for this was difficult and thorny; it led through its own Gethsemane and Calvary, in identification with the Christ of God. I also knew that this was the way I would have to go, though of course the outward circumstances might be very different. I saw that within the religious life or not, just one thing was needful: to enter into a contemplative love of God in Christ.[75] Here I was, on the edge of entering into community life, hungering for the life of prayer with its roots deep into the mystery of the divine love. And the Lord had brought me to a place where I could see, and feel, and know the reality, the power and the validity of a life dedicated to God in prayer.

The lamb of God
from *A Hidden Fire*

I had been living in solitude for nearly six months on the Lleyn Peninsula, facing the island of Bardsey, with mountain sheep scattered over the hillside above the sea. On Maundy Thursday, I climbed to the top of the hill Anelog, where there was a flat, exposed area. There I marked 14 stones with the 'Stations of the Cross', and a fifteenth mound of stones surmounted with an empty wooden cross for the resurrection.

So, on Good Friday I ascended the hill to walk the stations from 2.00 pm to 3.00 pm, following Jesus' way of sorrows to Calvary. It was windy, dark and menacing as I climbed the hill, and when I got to the top I found, in the midst of the 15 stations, a dead lamb. It had been attacked, blinded and killed by the ravens, and as I looked at its small, white woolly body among the rocks I was moved to tears, and said, 'O Lamb of God, who takes away the sins of the world, have mercy upon us...'

I prayed the stations of the cross through the next hour, and during that time the wind dropped, the clouds parted and the sun broke through. The dead lamb remained in the midst of the stones, but I was able to move from the death to the risen life of Jesus in the scriptures and in the events of the day, which were all taken up into my prayer.

The climb ahead
from *The Prayer Mountain*

I value solitude more than ever, though I am the first to confess that I owe a great deal to my community in enabling me to take this path, and to all those who have traversed this way before me. I am not alone, for I build on their teaching and experiences, and am increasingly aware of the communion of saints and angels who pray for me.

For me, this life is not the end of my life of witness and ministry, but the beginning of a new pilgrimage of prayer and love. And although solitude is the greater part of it, I am not alone. Not only am I surrounded by the prayers and influence of others on earth and in heaven, but I am making this journey for others, and for a world which is filled with loneliness, suffering and wickedness. It is a world of joy and glory too, and that is why I share my journey with others. The early Alpine climbing rope had a thread of red or scarlet running through its length. This speaks to me of the redeeming love of Christ, and it is the rope by which I climb, and which I hold out to others on the perilous and joyous slopes of our journey. We are all in it together, and although the shape of our mountain may vary, the same path of love and prayer leads us to the summit, which is participation in the love of God.

The longing heart
from *Forty Days and Forty Nights*

I am writing today in the solitude of a hermitage for you who may be harassed by the numerous demands of work, home, school, hospital, family, friends, financial pressure or unemployed forced leisure. Perhaps you may be one of those who lives out their own solitude in an unvisited flat or hospital bed, longing for someone to talk to, to confide in and to love. Or you may be so consumed by the incessant demands of relationships, home and work that you long for time and space to be alone.

Our situation may be radically different and yet the longing in our hearts may meet in mutual recognition. Before I came here I was surrounded, even in a monastery, by continual demands on time, energy, compassion and understanding. There were times when I longed for solitude at every level. And then it came.

Who knows where you may be in two or three years' time, what relationships may be severed, what dissolution or enhancement may have taken place in your life? We only have the time and place we find ourselves in today, and God asks for this moment with whatever weariness or joy accompanies it.

Mary of Bethany knelt before the Lord Jesus; she touched his feet in humble adoration; she heard his words of gentle commendation; she felt the flowing energy that communicated itself from his loving heart.

This is the kind of contemplative spirit of which Charles Wesley writes, and which is offered to you and me if we will yield ourselves completely to him:

> *O Love divine, how sweet thou art!*
> *When shall I find my longing heart*
> *All taken up by thee?*
> *I thirst, I faint and die to prove*
> *The greatness of redeeming love,*
> *The love of Christ to me.*

Trusting where I cannot see...
from *Forty Days and Forty Nights*

Over the years, I have learned to differentiate between the profound, basic sense of God's presence, and the emotional high that sometimes accompanies it. So there are times when the Lord says, 'Ramon, I am taking away those feelings and emotions which you so much enjoy, but you will retain an interior sense of my presence in the darkness and the struggle through which I require you to go.'

I understand that and accept it. Indeed, it is during such times that real growth takes place, without the emotional gratification which is absent during those periods.

But there is also the experience during which not only the feeling part of religion is denied but also *any* sense of God's loving presence – it is rather a feeling of absence. I am just left without any sign or evidence of his favour and presence. I am still learning to receive such periods, not with resignation or fear, but with the kind of acceptance that takes from God's hand just what he wills to give. I think it was Catherine of Siena who went through two years of desert aridity in her spiritual life. When she afterwards entered into joy she cried, 'Lord, where were you during that awful time?' And he answered, 'Catherine, I was not only with you, but sustained you in it all, else you would never have come through.' That's it – trusting where I cannot see; believing where I cannot prove.

The call to the hidden life
from *Deeper into God*

The members of our physical bodies serve particular functions within the unity of the organism. Some of them are communicating members, such as the eyes, the ears, the tongue, the hands and feet, as well as possessing other functions. But there are some members and organs which are vital and may not *seem* to communicate, in that they are not engaged in verbal or visible dialogue, but they have the primary function of sustaining life, and participate in the life-system in a hidden manner and are indispensable. The heart is such a vital organ, though it is symbolically associated with the communication of compassion and love. The liver is such an organ which cannot be seen, felt or 'experienced' by the layman. It is a hidden and vital organ which performs basic indispensable functions, but is not thought to be a communicative organ in the sense referred to above. So, in the body of Christ, there are those called to the hidden life, a vital life, a life of interior prayer which does not seem to have the communicative functions of proclamation, witness, dialogue or teaching. But their function is indispensable and vital to the living organism of the body of Christ. The principle of retreat and return for them is lived out at a deeper level of contemplative prayer. They are called into the desert to give themselves completely in a life of prayer and love to God alone.

Gethsemane
from *Forty Days and Forty Nights*

The solitude of Gethsemane was loneliness, for it was there that Jesus entered into the beginnings of his dereliction which was brought to its consummation in those fearful words from the cross: 'My God, my God, why have you forsaken me?' (Matthew 27:46). Already in Gethsemane, the disciples had forsaken him in spirit because they could not bear to face the harrowing loneliness of the deepening darkness which was engulfing them. And soon they would forsake him physically, for the crowd of soldiers and religionists led by Judas were already making their way to the olive grove. If Jesus ever needed human companionship and warmth, he needed it then, but 'all the disciples deserted him and fled'.

There is no comparison between my darkness and his, but we all have to share the same pilgrimage to Calvary that he undertook. The path the master walked must be followed by the servant, for though it is a path of suffering, it is also a path of love. And a share in the solitude and loneliness of Jesus is part of the pattern for every disciple.

The life that will not die
from *Fullness of Joy*

I write today before an upstairs window of the monastery at Glasshampton on a clear, crisp December day. There is a beautiful chestnut tree before me in the field beyond the laurel hedge. It stands stark and bare under the grey winter sky, with the ragged remnants of crisp, dried leaves clinging here and there, its branches moving rhythmically in the gentle wind. And I know that it contains a great secret within its centre, and that unseen, the root-network reaches deep down into the profound mystery of humus and darkness below. I know that it will maintain its silent and naked witness throughout the coming months of frost, ice and cold. It will be shaken by the winds, soaked by the rains, and stand a sentinel in the falling snow. I've seen it before. But I also know that the secret of springtime is locked within its being, and that when the time is right, the ground will soften, the year will turn, the warmth will come, the sun will shine. Then the sap will rise, unknown, unsuspected to the faithless eye, and the glory of resurrection will fulfil its yearly cycle and all the world will sing again.

This is the pattern of the gospel, reflected and re-enacted in my own spiritual life. When the Christian says, 'There is no death', he is not denying the mortal reality of physical dissolution, or the pain and sadness of bereavement and earthly loss. And he certainly cannot deny the awful reality of the immoral labour and concentration camps in which thousands of human beings have been, and are, thrust to a premature and horrific death. But what he is affirming is the eternal dimension, the love that knows no end, the life that will not die. And what he is denying is that death has any *ultimate* power, any reality of its own, any rootedness in the eternal order in which the victory remains with love. It is from the gospel perspective that the apostle cried out with great gladness:

> Death is swallowed up in victory
> O death, where is thy victory?
> O death, where is thy sting?
> 1 CORINTHIANS 15:54–55

Immanence and transcendence
from *The Listening Heart*

God is transcendent, above and beyond this world of time and space, but he is also immanent, dwelling at the heart of the created order.

The very breath which we breathe, the spring sap which rises in the trees, the creative pulse which causes the sun to rise and set, the moon to wax and wane, the seas to ebb and flow – this is the manifestation of the immanence of God. In other words, of the Holy Spirit, the Lord and life-giver. The more we become aware of the dynamic life within the communion of the Holy Trinity, the more we shall understand the experience of both the transcendence and immanence of God.

As I write these words, they are set within a day in which I spent some hours digging and caring for the monastery vegetable garden, and that involves me in meditation of the divine indwelling in nature. It not only possesses me in the inwardness of my own spirituality, but is in the very earth which I turn over with my spade. I pierce the earth in order to plant seed potatoes. The awareness of sun, moisture and warm air makes me reflect upon the creative womb of the earth which will nurture the buried seed until it germinates, bursts forth above the ground and reaches up towards sun, sky and the bearing of fruit. I am also aware of the masculine and feminine analogies implicit in all this cooperative activity, and the whole wonder of the immanence of God brings me close to tears. And running alongside this as a sort of counterpoint, in parallel and complement, is the appearance of the Pantocrator in the Apocalypse.

If I trembled in wonder, gentleness and tears at the experience of God's immanence, I am now confronted with his transcendence – the God who is and who was and who is to come, the Almighty.

Confronting solitude
from *Praying the Jesus Prayer Together*

After I had spent six positive months of spring and summer solitude in Dorset in the early 1980s, I sensed a pressing call to repeat it a year or so later. Mother Mary Clare SLG was then my spiritual director and she gently but insistently guided me towards this more demanding confrontation with my own solitude, the next step to what eventually became a hermit vocation. As a contrast to the first gentle period of solitude, I now needed wild mountain terrain, bleak cold days and nights with winds, storms and heaving sea reflecting winter's heaviness, darkness and mystery. This landed me on the tip of the Lleyn peninsular on the North Wales coast, facing the powerful island of Bardsey, the 'island of 20,000 saints' – tiny as it is – where, in medieval times, three pilgrimages there were worth one to Jerusalem. I wrote to Mother Mary Clare in my first report from there:

> Darkness and mist fall over the mountain, the cry of the high wind echoes around the cottage and the dim outlines of the surrounding rocky heights bear witness to the austerity of the months to come. But the mystic fire burns within, and the longing for the Beloved and the pain of absence mingle in the way that opens before me.

As to Bardsey itself, it served to underline my solitude and solidarity with all the people on earth and within the communion of saints. Sometimes the facing island loomed dark and menacing out of the turbulent waters. Sometimes it would catch and reflect the glorious sunset over still and golden sea. But always, as the island of 20,000 saints, it possessed a quality of the numinous, of awe and mystery – and a spiritual quality that was threatening as well as glorious. I felt the peninsula in its pagan as well as its Christian setting. The whole feel of the place not only changed with my changing moods, but I felt that it sometimes imposed its own mood upon me... It was in this place that the Jesus Prayer ministered to me in preparation for further evolution of my vocation.

Sharing my way
from part of a Lent Talk for BBC Radio Devon, March 1985

All our paths of prayer are different, and I don't expect people to walk *my* way, though I would share my way which may shed its own light on your path.

Over the last four or five years, I have been drawn more and more into the prayer of solitude, which, in fact, has made me more and not less aware of my place in the body of Christ, and of our common humanity.

Therefore on two occasions, supported by the prayer of my Franciscan brothers and sisters, I have gone into the wilderness for two six-month periods of solitude in the depths of Dorset in a thickly wooded area, during a beautiful spring and summer. In the autumn and winter of 1983–84, I lived in a small stone cottage on a mountain on the edge of the Welsh Lleyn Peninsula, facing the island of Bardsey.

The first period of solitude was full of light and glory, of ecstasy and beauty, with a patch of psychical and spiritual darkness in the midst of it. The second period was exposure to much more darkness, in which I was thrown upon the mercy and love of God in the midst of spiritual conflict.

For me, the whole dimension of prayer was the most real, the most aware of a call, a compulsion, a yearning for the divine love.

In the wilderness, there was no one to impress, no images to project, no spectacular, clever, intellectual or spiritual ministry to stimulate my hyperactivity. Only myself and God. I became aware of the cosmic processes of nature and grace, more aware of the movement of God in earth, sea and sky, in nature and in my very self…

I found gospel scenes drawing me into identification of myself with the characters of the gospel story. I was a leper who came to Jesus for cleansing; I was John the Baptist incarcerated in a prison cell; I was John the beloved disciple at the foot of the cross; I was Mary, dear mother of our Lord, weeping – her heart pierced by the sword of sorrow and suffering.

Questions for reflection or discussion

1 Ramon values quiet places where he is aware of God's presence. Can you find a quiet space, a room, a church, a park or the countryside where you can sense the presence of God in the beauty that surrounds you and where you can rest in his peace free from all pressures and stress?

2 Solitude is one of the great themes of Jesus' teaching. 'Go into your room and shut the door', he says. 'Pray to your Father who is in secret; and your Father who sees in secret will reward you' (Matthew 6:6). Can you find time in a busy life to be alone with God and enjoy the silence?

3 Meditate on Psalm 139:1–17. Listen to what God is saying to you in these words.

4 If you have never been on a retreat but feel the need for a period of silence for a day, a week or even longer, speak to your minister/priest about the possibility. (See 'Why retreat?', p. 143.)

5 What does it mean for *you* to be a member of the body of Christ? What do you see as your particular function or ministry? (See 'Belonging together', p. 144.)

Living faith: in the world

Open-minded or compromising?
from *My Questions – God's Questions*

I have always had a wide spectrum of Christian friends, but many of them, in my early days, would not have dreamed of relating to a Buddhist, Sikh or Hindu, even if there had been the opportunity. There was even great caution in being friendly to a Jew, unless you witnessed to Christ as Messiah! What I did find especially suspect (recognising it as spiritual blackmail?) was the encouraging of friendliness to non-Christians in order to win them for Christ!

Some of my friends were so conservative they believed in 'guarding' their pulpit and the Holy Communion, lest someone should deviate from *their* interpretation of the Bible or receive Communion while not in *their* fellowship.

I find it all so fantastic now and certainly found it counterproductive then, for I reacted against it. And yet, although I rejoice in the openness and freedom which I practise among all the people of God now, I know there were many sincere and devoted people among the fundamentalists I've mentioned. If you ever belonged to such a group, you will know how much courage it takes to stand against the party line, and how difficult it is to break away from such religious bondage.

But where does all this leave us? Well, sometimes we have to be pastorally right even if we are theologically wrong! So I would encourage you to be open and loving in all your relationships, while not swallowing a vacuous theology which is neither Catholic nor Evangelical. There are stands to be made, both theologically and morally, and while we may be compassionate in all our dealings, we should not be shoddy and inconsistent when the issues are serious.

To be capable of love
from *Forty Days and Forty Nights*

To be capable of love is a very precious, a very human potentiality. If you have found your own depths moved in love, then be thankful and let your joy spill over the boundaries of your own life. It begins with a sheer gift of grace, a warm flow of life and energy that enables you to love your deepest self in response to the love which embraces you on every side. Parental love can be received and reciprocated, and from such a vantage point of security and warmth you will be able to demonstrate love for the inanimate created order, for the animal creation, for friends, neighbours and strangers. And then to fall in love… to give yourself to another and to be received in love. All this is a training ground for the love of God to flow and overflow, so that you will be able to love the poor, the weak, the oppressed and the ugly… to love those who cannot or will not return your love… and to love those who hate and persecute you.

And where is the origin, the inspiration and source of such love? It is in God.

The cost of forgiveness
from *My Questions, God's Questions*

Out of the many scriptures which strive to portray the meaning of the cross, there is this beautiful text: 'In Christ God was reconciling the world to himself, not counting their trespasses against them, and entrusting the message of reconciliation to us' (2 Corinthians 5:19).

In Old Testament days it was thought that, in some mysterious way, the high priest could transfer the sins of the people to the scapegoat and then drive it out into the wilderness of desolation to die; or that he could lay the sins upon a sacrificial lamb so that its blood could somehow atone for sin. Such blood sacrifices could never cleanse away sin (Hebrews 10:4); but when John the Baptist bore witness to Jesus, he said, 'Here is the lamb of God who takes away the sin of the world' (John 1:29). Christ is the fulfilment of all the types and yearnings of Old Testament piety, for it is by his reconciling work that God showed the depth of his love and the extent of his mercy to us.

The top of the cross reaches right into the tender heart of God; the base of the cross reaches down to the lowest depth of hell to which humankind could ever sink; the arms of the cross reach out to all people everywhere. God, incarnate in Christ, dies upon the cross, and because he is God, rises from death's power and penalty to become our risen Saviour and Lord. One of the loveliest prayers at the Eucharist puts it like this:

> He opened wide his arms for us on the cross;
> He put an end to death by dying for us
> And revealed the resurrection by rising to new life.

There is a great deal more to it... But although God could have received our repentance and faith, and forgiven us outright and simply, he desired to show us how much our sin cost him, and how much he tenderly loves us – even to the end. So look upon the cross and be filled with tears, with love and with joy.

On fasting
from *Forty Days and Forty Nights*

Christianity, with its roots in Judaism, commended personal and communal fasting... For me, not only is it a token of repentance and participation with the fasting, sorrowing Jesus, but it unites me with the prophetic and apostolic tradition, with the ascetic athletes of the desert, and gives me a sense of solidarity with the suffering church and world in these days of violence, hunger, persecution and deprivation.

We all need a faith which has backbone and an element of sacrifice in it. The gospel is meant to be a source of comfort and shelter in time of weakness and need, but it is no tranquilliser or opium to lull us into a false security while the major part of the world is experiencing hell.

We are all aware of the surfeit of superfluous goods in the 'developed' world which encourages destruction of crops and harvests to keep prices and demand up while gross malnutrition leads most 'underdeveloped' countries to death. And we are continually exposed to the advertising media's manic efforts to create further 'needs' for unnecessary products in such a mad world.

This theme of fasting is not meant to pile guilt but rather to encourage us in the joy of sacrifice on our part, personally and communally, which pays dividends elsewhere. If you take this path, your body will become healthier and you will appreciate basic and nourishing food all the more.

The cycle of love
from *Forty Days and Forty Nights*

God has ordered the natural cycle of seasons according to a pattern of variety and change, design and fruitfulness. So we find reflected in our inner lives a seasonal and spiritual cycle which promotes our good and God's glory. Springtime captures all those moments of new life and hope which burst forth in the soul – the rising of the sap, the putting forth of buds and blossom, the anticipation of beauty and wonder. Summer encapsulates the full glory of awakened energies, the fulfilment of early hopes and longings and the long days of joyful labour and happy relationships.

Autumn pictures the ripening and gathering of maturing fruitfulness, the maturity of wise counsel and experience, and the joyfulness of work well done. Winter brings the cold blasts of declining days, the falling of the sap and the acceptance of a good and gentle death.

Yet, for the believer, even in the freezing winter season the bright shoots of spring are already stirring in the deep soil of the soul. The changing of the seasons is the rhythmic movement of God's Spirit in the earth, reflected in the body, mind and spirit of human life.

Eat, drink and be merry?
from *The Way of Love*

In our contemporary marketplace, economy, finance dictates our every move – from the water we drink to super-expensive geriatric care and funerals which are an increasing source of worry for elderly people for years before they die. The accountant looms behind health, education and basic needs of warmth and shelter. The increasingly sad (but not new) scandal is the chasm between those who earn astronomical salaries and those who sleep in the streets and are ineligible for even basic survival allowance.

A little while ago, as a visiting friar, I concluded a sermon to a church congregation which got me some peculiar looks when I said, 'I know many of you haven't two pennies to rub together – but there are some of you who would not miss a thousand pounds or two from your bank balance. I'll tell you what I'd like you to do this week – send £100 to some needy family in your area. Don't think too long about it, just do it!' I wonder if any of them did?

The strange thing is that we always want a bit more. It was Seneca, I believe, who said, 'Money is like sea water – the more you drink, the thirstier you become.' My mother had a good answer to such an attitude: 'There are no pockets in shrouds!'…

The gospel is not a negative set of 'don'ts'. Neither is it a teaching majoring on asceticism or mortification as a way of life. Jesus' offer was of life in all its fullness, and if he preached self-sacrifice (which he did), it was to cast off the second-best in order to achieve the best; a letting-go of the superfluous, hindering obstacles that cheat and deceive us, in order that we might enter into a simpler, happier, more open and loving way of existing. Nevertheless, there is a call to strip down excesses. It is a call to spiritual health, or even spiritual athleticism. In order to gain mastery, or win the prize, there is the discipline, the asceticism of surrendering the superfluous – for your own sake and the sake of others.

Christ in Francis
from *Franciscan Spirituality*

Francis entered into union with Christ in love. In such a life, he suffered in and with Christ, took to himself the pains and sorrows of his brothers and sisters, and then confronted the powers of darkness at their source. This is what the gospel meant to Francis, and that is what it must mean to us.

Christ becomes incarnate in the believer, and the way in which our response to God's call is lived out becomes our personal vocation. For some, it will be an apostolic life of preaching and prayer; for others, a mystical life of contemplation. For some, it will be a missionary call to the ends of the earth... for others, it will be a faithful living out of home, family, and involvement with agencies of compassion, peace and justice. Life stories may vary greatly, but all God's people are called to incarnate Christ in the world.

The powers of light and darkness
from *The Listening Heart*

The New Testament is very clear that there are powers of light and darkness behind the forces which are manifested in our world. It is not dualistic, for there is no doubt about the outcome – for the divine love will overcome all obstacles at the last. But while history runs its course the conflict rages, and behind peoples and nations there are ranged dark powers of evil (see Ephesians 6:11–12).

There are dangers in an over-literal interpretation of scripture, especially in the Apocalypse, which abounds in angels and demons, and which can result in the present charismatic fascination with occult powers in a fundamentalist mode. This not only gives rise to the writing of fantastic novels of over 500 pages, where the 'Captain of the Angelic Host' zooms around zapping all and sundry, but can result in the evasion of our own responsibility by laying the causes of all sin and sickness at the devil's door.

The New Testament writers do not do this. They acknowledge the reality of the angelic and demonic dimensions, but make human responsibility a primary response to God's demand for righteousness and justice.

There is such a thing as dark, cosmic conflict; there are dark powers behind warring nations, and such powers are not simply psychic, but have a more objective reality and influence. But our response to such a dimension of reality is that we should be concerned with the sovereignty of God, allying ourselves with loving compassion and prayerful watchfulness. The battle for good against evil will not be won by taking up carnal weapons or engaging in national or religious conflicts, but by the continual yielding of ourselves, as individuals and churches, to the non-violent witness of reconciliation and peace-making wherever there is a battlefield and wherever human rights are betrayed at any level.

The sun and the cross
from *Franciscan Spirituality*

These are the two images contained in the Franciscan synthesis – the sun and the cross. The sun represents Francis in relation to the created order – every creature is brother, sister and mother within the maternal and paternal fatherhood of God.

But Francis knows that we do not live in an Edenic paradise. Sin has invaded the world and its peoples, producing enmity, separation and disintegration. The unity has been ruptured; humanity has fallen from grace and broken the covenant and heart of God. Therefore the cross is indispensable in bridging the chasm caused by sin. God's broken heart has been revealed in his incarnation among his people. He has borne their griefs and carried their sorrows in the death and resurrection of Christ.

By way of the cross, the sun rises again in the heart of the believer. The lost Eden is restored and paradise regained. By this synthesis of sun and cross, a double blessing is experienced. Fallen humanity is reconciled to God, and the broken world is integrated again into a cosmic unity, so that the blessings of the future kingdom are tasted now, and the powers of the world to come are already anticipated.

This sets the scene for the practical outworking of the synthesis. The sun represents the ecological dimensions of our social and political lives. The cross represents the relational aspects of communal structures, national and international. In other words, a Franciscan spirituality commits the believer to cosmic renewal in all tasks that go towards building a purified and renewed world on the one hand, and the work of forgiveness and reconciliation that builds up redeemed relationships throughout the world on the other...

Like Francis, we have to repair the ruins with bricks and mortar, and we have to forgive and help our brothers and sisters with compassion and healing.

Complaining
from *Forty Days and Forty Nights*

It is difficult for a parish priest or clergy team when they have to minister to people who are continually complaining, for these people are often the same ones who complain to their local doctor, medical panel or parent-teacher association. Nothing goes right for them, everyone opposes them and the world is set against them. And because of their constant carping, their gloomy predictions are often self-fulfilling, for people begin to avoid them. Of course, sometimes it is the fault of the parish priest, the local doctor or the awkward teacher, but if there are difficult professional men and women these people will find them.

It's an old problem, because when God walked in the garden of Eden in the cool of the day he called, 'Adam, where are you?' As soon as the guilty pair turned up, he blamed her, she blamed the serpent and that's where the buck stopped (Genesis 3:8–14).

There are times, dear Lord, when we are angry with ourselves because our lives are not fulfilling their potential; we are angry with our loved ones and friends because they do not understand us; we are angry with you because you have made us as we are.

Help us to pour out our complaints honestly before you, to see clearly what it is that causes our anger to erupt and to come to terms with the reality of our lives;

Through Jesus Christ, our Lord. Amen.

Being truthful and open
from *The Listening Heart*

And who is neighbour? Well, Samaritan or Jew, Catholic or Quaker, Buddhist or Sikh; and we are increasingly realising that the voices of the oppressed and violated animals and the ecological balance of the world are included, and are our responsibility...

It is a matter of becoming loving and open to all people, and this extends to sentient creatures, and ultimately to the whole of creation. It is a lifelong task, but is the way of Jesus... I am not suggesting that we sink our profoundly held beliefs in an indifferent tolerance that holds nothing distinctively precious and basic. Such a religion, apart from not being worth anything, would certainly not produce martyrs! What we must do is tune our hearts and minds to the risen Christ, the centre of our faith. We must hold the essential truths of our revealed faith precious – for it is a faith to die for – and to live for. But above all, we must remember that this is not a religion of dogmatic propositions, but the revelation of God's love in Christ.

I do not water down the amazing revelation of the divinity of Christ when I dialogue with a Buddhist friend. I do not belittle Christ's deity to fit the measure of a human prophet, charismatic guru or healer. I commend Christ the Saviour in all his fullness – but I also listen to my Buddhist friend and appreciate the words of wisdom he has to share with me. The outcome is that he enters into an understanding of Christ's compassion, and I discover the hidden Christ in so much of what he has to share. This is not compromise but dialogue, and even if we disagree it is in the spirit of seeking truth.

Beloved disciple
from *When They Crucified My Lord*

Picture Jesus reclining with his disciples at the last supper, with the beloved disciple reclining close to his heart. The text actually says *en to kolpotoulesou*: in the bosom of Jesus (John 13:21–26). The word *kolpos,* breast or bosom, is the very word used of Jesus dwelling in the intimate heart of the Father, 'in the bosom of the Father' (John 1:18). The relation of the disciple to his Saviour is likened to that of the Son to the Father. This is mystical indwelling which is at the heart of spirituality as presented in John's Gospel, in which the believer dwells within the bosom of the Son, and the Son dwells within the bosom of the believer. This is to be seen within the context of a wider Trinitarian mysticism in which the believer and the church participate in the very life of the Trinity, and is already pictured in this passage.

The upper room is heavy with sorrow as Jesus is troubled in spirit, and he causes a profound stirring of curious grief when he says, 'Very truly, I tell you, one of you will betray me.' By simple action (a nod, says the Greek text), Peter indicates to John that he should ask Jesus of whom he was speaking, for all the disciples felt the enshrouding darkness and pain that accompanied the words and spirit of Jesus.

John was the only one who could ask such a question at such a time, and again close attention to the text indicates the intimacy of the moment, for it says, literally, 'falling back on the breast of Jesus, he says to him, "Lord, who is it?"' John is able to enter into that secret place, to ask the most intimate question, to share the profoundest grief and to receive the most secret word of Jesus.

The whole process of 'falling back' into the secret place indicates that what Jesus says is not for public hearing, not for the world, not even for the other disciples, but for John alone... 'John the disciple leaned on the breast of Jesus, and felt the very heartbeat of God.'

The joy of God
from *Fullness of Joy*

There is a stupendous claim made in the second letter of Peter which is consonant with the rest of the New Testament – that we are 'partakers of the divine nature' (2 Peter 1:4, ESV). We share the very life of God. And one of the chief manifestations of that life is joy. If you take up a concordance and trace the various expressions of lively joy, it will become clear that they all have their source in God himself. It is not simply that there is a certain joy in recognising his creative and redemptive claim upon human life, nor merely that there is a simply human joy in adoration and worship – but that human joy which is rooted in righteousness and compassion, and often overflows in an infusion of spiritual inebriation, finds God as its very source. Joy is the upsurge and overflow of the divine life in nature and in human experience.

At creation, we are told that the morning stars sang together and all the sons of God shouted for sheer joy, and in the redemption of a single sinner we are assured that there is joy in the presence of the angels (Job 38:7; Luke 15:7, 10). For that reason, we are able with joy to draw water from the wells of salvation (Isaiah 12:3), for the Bible attributes joy to the Father, the Son and the Holy Spirit (Nehemiah 8:10; John 15:11; Romans 14:17; 1Thessalonians 1:6).

Scriptures of the Old and New Testaments display an embarrassing richness of joyful testimony, directly and indirectly bearing witness to the joy which overflows from the bounty of the Godhead, streaming from the mountains of creation and the springs of redemption. This is confirmation of the experience of joy which may be directly perceived in creation, and is basic to the created order, in contrast to the melancholy sadness which is the temporary and intermediate state of our present existence. The promise is that, though weeping may endure for a night, joy comes in the morning, and that though sowing may be in tears and hope, the harvest will be fulfilment and consummation in joy (Psalm 30:5; 126:5, 6).

Ecumenical spirituality
from *The Flame of Sacred Love*

There is only one church of God, and it is a cause of great sadness that our denominational divisions do not reflect our one Lord, one faith and one baptism. But these are also ecumenical days, and that very word ecumenical means 'household' of faith. There is an increasing amount of sharing between the communions of Christ's church, and wide-ranging consensus among theologians and liturgical practice. If I were to offer a retreat under the title 'A Christian Spirituality for Today', I would quite likely have among the retreatants, Anglicans, Baptists, Brethren, Catholics, Methodists, New (House) Churches, Pentecostals, Quakers, Salvationists, URCs, and perhaps (because they are thinner on the ground) one or two Lutherans and Orthodox.

There is quite likely to be a Baptist wanting to make his confession, a Methodist fingering at the Jesus Prayer rope, a Quaker asking if she can share the Eucharist and a Catholic and Methodist sharing the laying-on-of-hands and anointing of the sick.

I would like to feel that we are all looking forward towards Vincent of Lérins' famous formula of the basic content of the Christian faith: 'That which has been believed everywhere, always and by all.' He did not mean that to be a rigid or dogmatic definition because he goes on to affirm that 'there should be a great increase and vigorous progress in the individual as well as in the entire church as the ages and the centuries march on, of understanding, knowledge and wisdom'.

Were you there?
from *When They Crucified My Lord*

Poor Pilate is caught up in a web of political and religious machin-
ations, pulled in different directions. He was persuaded of Jesus'
innocence, for it was clear that here was no violent revolutionary,
yet he was paralysed in the face of a fanatical religious mob and the
state machine. At the end of the narrative (Matthew 27:11–26), we
find him crying out, 'What should I do with Jesus?' But it is not simply
a question for Pilate, where the roles were reversed in the judgement
hall, but also for you and for me. 'Were you there?' is the question
which will be continually asked of us, and the answer is, 'Yes, I was
there.' Indeed, it is not a historical question, but a present, existential
question which demands an answer today…

How easy it is for us, looking back, to condemn Pilate, to blame the
authorities, or to participate in the anti-Semitism which makes the
Jewish people responsible for the death of Jesus.

'Were you there?'

The answer is 'Yes'. So what will you do with Jesus?

Heaven is now…
from *The Flame of Sacred Love*

If I approach the living presence of God through scripture, through
sacrament and through prayer, I am brought into spiritual renewal;
if I need clarity of mind for the things of God, I ask for the Spirit's
illumination; if I suffer in sickness or infirmity, I seek through
charismatic and sacramental healing the anointing and healing of
the Spirit (James 5:13–16).

Thus heaven can begin today in my soul; eternal life is already rooted
within me; I already have glimpses of the prayer of quiet and the
unitive life which is the life of heaven.

If such a holistic experience of salvation is manifest among the people of God, then the effects will be felt first of all within the community of faith. Then it will spread to the surrounding community of family, friends and neighbourhood, reaching out into the world of suffering, injustice and conflict.

Questions for reflection or discussion

1 St Augustine said that 'God gives where he finds empty hands'. Our response is often, 'I'm sorry but my hands are full at the moment.' How might you set about emptying your hands and making room for God to act through you in today's world?

2 How important do you think it is to follow Ramon's example and have dialogue and make friends not only with Christians of other traditions, but people of other faiths? How does your church encourage people with different backgrounds to share their faith and develop friendships? (See 'Open-minded or compromising?', p. 155.)

3 How can the church best witness to the generosity of God in an acquisitive society? (See 'On fasting', p. 157.)

4 'We all need a faith which has backbone and an element of sacrifice in it.' Can you think of ways in which you can practise fasting or self-denial in your life (See 'Eat, drink and be merry', p. 159.)

5 Ramon speaks about the conflict between light and darkness and good and evil. How do you cope with darkness in your life and in the life of the world? (See 'The powers of light and darkness', p. 160.)

Books by Brother Ramon

Marshall Pickering

- *A Hidden Fire* (1985)
- *Deeper into God* (1987)
- *Life's Changing Seasons* (1988)
- *Remember Me* (1988)
- *Soul Friends* (1989)
- *Forty Days and Forty Nights* (1993)
- *The Heart of Prayer* (1995)
- *The Listening Heart* (1996)
- *Fullness of Joy* (1998)

SPCK

- *Franciscan Spirituality* (1994)
- *My Questions, God's Answers* (1998)
- *A Month with St Francis* (1999)

BRF

- *The Flame of Sacred Love* (1999)
- *When They Crucified My Lord* (1999)
- *Praying the Jesus Prayer Together* (2001)

HarperCollins

- *Jacapone* (1990)
- *Heaven on Earth* (1991)
- *The Way of Love* (1995)

Lion Publishing

- *The Wisdom of St Francis* (1997)

Canterbury Press

- *The Prayer Mountain* (1998)

Ligouri Publications

- *Seven Days in Solitude* (2000)

Notes

1 Brother Ramon, *Forty Days and Forty Nights* (Marshall Pickering, 1993), p. 152.
2 *The Franciscan* (January 1998).
3 *Forty Days and Forty Nights,* p. 236.
4 Brother Ramon, *A Hidden Fire* (Marshall Pickering, 1985), p. 21.
5 *A Hidden Fire,* p. 21.
6 *A Hidden Fire,* p. 29.
7 Brother Ramon, *Fullness of Joy* (Marshall Pickering, 1998), p. 95.
8 *Fullness of Joy,* pp. 96–97.
9 *Fullness of Joy,* pp. 97.
10 *Baptist Times* ('He was an evangelical whirlwind', 27 July 2000).
11 *Baptist Times* ('He was an evangelical whirlwind', 27 July 2000).
12 *The Voice* (14 August 1959).
13 I am grateful to Ron Powell for this quotation. He adds: 'I see in that and other statements a shift in his theology and a growing interest in the Anglican family in his choice of John Robinson as a subject.'
14 'Benediction of the Blessed Sacrament': a liturgy at which the consecrated bread of the Eucharist is lifted up before the congregation as a blessing from Christ's sacramental presence.
15 *A Hidden Fire,* p. 25.
16 Words used in the introduction in the Marriage Service.
17 A.H. Allchin (ed.), *Solitude and Communion: Papers on the hermit life given at St David's* (Fairacres Publications, 1997).
18 *Fullness of Joy,* p. 24.
19 Brother Ramon, *The Heart of Prayer* (Marshall Pickering, 1995), p. 9.
20 Brother Ramon, *Franciscan Spirituality* (SPCK, 1994), p. 13.
21 *The Scotsman* (11 April 2011). Father Walls later joined the Roman Catholic Church.
22 *The Heart of Prayer,* p. 63.
23 Brother Ramon, *Soul Friends: A journey with Thomas Merton* (Marshall Pickering, 1989) is based on this research.
24 I am most grateful to Brother James Halsey, brother in charge of Roslin, for this information.
25 Brother Ramon, *The Prayer Mountain* (Canterbury Press, 1998), p. 14.
26 *Soul Friends,* p. x.

27 *Soul Friends,* p. xi.
28 Brother Ramon, *The Flame of Sacred Love* (BRF, 1999), p. 79.
29 William H. Shannon, *Thomas Merton's Dark Path* (Collins, 1987), p. 7.
30 Shannon, *Thomas Merton's Dark Path,* p. 137.
31 Brother Ramon, *A Month with Saint Francis* (SPCK, 1999), p. 12.
32 Letter to Ronald, Ann, Chris, Angela and Jonathan (undated).
33 Letter to Ron (undated).
34 *A Hidden Fire,* p. 42.
35 Letter to Ron, Annie and family (October 1982).
36 Letter to Ron, Annie and family (October 1982).
37 Letter to Ron, Annie and family (October 1982).
38 *A Hidden Fire,* p. 23.
39 David G.R. Keller (ed.), *Boundless Grandeur: The Christian vision of A. M. Donald Allchin* (Pickwick Publications, 2015), p. 144.
40 Andrew Jones, *Pilgrimage* (BRF, 2001), p. 186.
41 Sister Mary Clare was a member of the Anglican contemplative Community of the Love of God at Fairacres, Oxford where SSF brothers acted as chaplains and where, from 1968–73, Donald Allchin had been warden.
42 *A Hidden Fire,* p. 52.
43 *A Hidden Fire,* p. 56.
44 The 'Dark Night of the Soul' is a phrase which occurs in a poem by St John of the Cross (1542–91), a Spanish mystic. He applied it to the monk who seeks God and who finds that in so doing he must pass through the experience of Christ's passion, Gethsemane and the cross – a prelude to the resurrection and the vision of Christ's glory.
45 *Fullness of Joy,* p. 186.
46 *A Hidden Fire,* p. 54.
47 *A Hidden Fire,* p. 57.
48 *A Hidden Fire,* p. 54–55.
49 Letter to Ron: Anelog (16 November 1983).
50 For a full account of the history of the Society of the Sacred Cross, see *Continuous Miracle* published by Tymawr Convent.
51 *Forty Days and Forty Nights,* p. 18.
52 Letter to Ron: Tymawr (31 December 1990).
53 Letter to Ron (19 December 1992).
54 Letter to Ron (2 March 1993).
55 Letter to Ron (2 March 1993).
56 Letter to Ron: Glasshampton (15 October 1993).
57 Francis Ridley Havergal was born at Astley and died at Caswell, Swansea – Ramon's home town.

58 *The Heart of Prayer,* p. 22.
59 *A Hidden Fire,* p. 68.
60 *A Hidden Fire,* p. 67.
61 Brother Ramon, *Deeper into God* (Marshall Pickering, 1987), p. 16.
62 *Deeper into God,* p. 9.
63 *Guidelines* (January–April 2002) (BRF, 2002).
64 Brother Ramon and Simon Barrington-Ward, *Praying the Jesus Prayer Together* (BRF, 2001), p. 119.
65 Letter to the author (7 March 1999).
66 Simon Barrington-Ward, *The Jesus Prayer* (BRF, 1996).
67 *Praying the Jesus Prayer Together,* pp. 26–27.
68 *Praying the Jesus Prayer Together,* pp. 91–92.
69 *Praying the Jesus Prayer Together,* p. 56.
70 *Praying the Jesus Prayer Together,* p. 31.
71 *Wesley's Hymns* (1779), p. 49.
72 Thomas of Celano, *The First Life of St Francis,* p. 83, quoted in Brother Ramon, *The Wisdom of St Francis* (Lion Publishing, 1997), p. 13.
73 Paul Tillich makes much of the New Testament distinction between the two words for time, *chronos* (clock time), and *kairos* (the moment of decision, maturity and readiness).
74 Ramon Lull, *The Book of the Lover and the Beloved,* Meditation 59 (SPCK, 1978).
75 Ramon is writing about the Hermit Symposium at St David's in 1975.

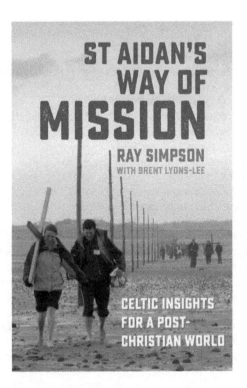

Surveying the life and times of Aidan of Lindisfarne, this book draws insights into missional approaches to inspire both outreach and discipleship for today's church. As in his previous BRF book, *Hilda of Whitby*, Ray Simpson shows that such figures from past centuries can provide models for Christian life and witness today. An author and speaker on Celtic spirituality with a worldwide reputation, he combines historical fact with spiritual lessons in a highly accessible style, with an appeal to a wide audience.

St Aidan's Way of Mission
Celtic insights for a post-Christian world
Ray Simpson
978 0 85746 485 9 £7.99

brfonline.org.uk

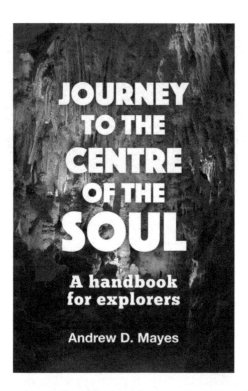

This unique and groundbreaking book is a summons to a subterranean spiritual adventure, an odyssey of the soul. If you let it, it will invigorate and inspire a search for something deeper in the spiritual life, and will link you with trusted spiritual guides to support you as you progress in a journey of discovery. *Journey to the Centre of the Soul* mines the rich seams of Christian spirituality, risks the depths, faces the darkness and make astonishing, transformative discoveries.

Journey to the Centre of the Soul
A handbook for explorers
Andrew D. Mayes
978 0 85746 582 5 £8.99

brfonline.org.uk

BRF

Transforming
lives and communities

Christian growth and understanding of the Bible

Resourcing individuals, groups and leaders in churches for their own spiritual journey and for their ministry

Church outreach in the local community

Offering three programmes that churches are embracing to great effect as they seek to engage with their local communities and transform lives

Teaching Christianity in primary schools

Working with children and teachers to explore Christianity creatively and confidently

Children's and family ministry

Working with churches and families to explore Christianity creatively and bring the Bible alive

Visit **brf.org.uk** for more information on BRF's work

brf.org.uk